Chauncey Giles

The sanctity of marriage

Chauncey Giles

The sanctity of marriage

ISBN/EAN: 9783741145919

Manufactured in Europe, USA, Canada, Australia, Japa

Cover: Foto ©Thomas Meinert / pixelio.de

Manufactured and distributed by brebook publishing software
(www.brebook.com)

Chauncey Giles

The sanctity of marriage

THE

SANCTITY OF MARRIAGE

BY THE

REV. CHAUNCEY GILES

AUTHOR OF "THE NATURE OF SPIRIT," "THE INCARNATION AND
ATONEMENT," "HEAVENLY BLESSEDNESS," ETC.

PHILADELPHIA

AMERICAN NEW-CHURCH TRACT AND PUBLICATION
SOCIETY

1129 CHESTNUT STREET

1896

CONTENTS.

THE

SANCTITY OF MARRIAGE.

I.

THE ORIGIN, NATURE, AND SANCTITY OF MARRIAGE.

*" So God created man in his own image, in the image of
God created he him ; male and female created he them."*—
GENESIS i. 27.

MARRIAGE, in common with many other subjects which touch the personal happiness and
vital interests of man and woman, is attracting
new and general attention. This movement is in
accordance with the universal laws of human
progress. We are impelled by the evils we suffer,
and allured by the hope of gaining more light and
attaining greater happiness, to seek for new truth
and devise new methods for a better organization
of society. This process must go on until we

find the ground of all human relations in the immutable laws of the Divine order. There is no other way of settling any question of human life and destiny. This principle applies in a most intimate and specific manner to the relations between man and woman. There is a common perception that they are the most intimate relations that one human being can hold to another ; that they are not merely formal, artificial, and determined by legislative power, but that they grow out of the specific nature of man and woman ; that marriage has its source and sanction in a power higher and prior to any human authority. But there is diversity of opinion upon the subject, and the origin and nature of marriage are not generally understood.

If we turn to the revelation which the Lord has made to man in the Sacred Scriptures, we find the origin and nature of marriage distinctly declared in the creation of man. " And God said, Let us make man in our image, after our likeness : and let them have dominion over the fish of the sea, and over the fowl of the air, and over the cattle, and over all the earth, and over every creeping thing that creepeth upon the earth. So God created man in his own image, in the image of God created he him ; male and female created he them." Our Lord, in His answer to the Pharisees concerning divorce, refers to this passage in Genesis and confirms its special application to marriage. "Have ye not read," He said, "that he which made them at the beginning made them male and female? and said, For this cause shall a man leave father and mother, and shall cleave to his wife ; and they twain shall be one flesh? Wherefore they are no more twain, but one flesh. What therefore God hath joined together, let not man put asunder."

In these words the important truth is revealed that man was created in the image and after the likeness of God,—that is, that the attributes of the Divine nature are finited in man. In the beginning man derived his essential nature from God. This truth applies to every human being. Every man begins in God. The first steps in his creation and the essential elements of his nature, unstained by evil and unperverted by error, are derived from God. Man inherits all his intellectual faculties and moral qualities from God according to the universal laws of heredity, as every seed inherits its qualities from the plant that bore it, every animal derives its form and nature from its parents, and every child its nature from its father and mother. When we call the Lord our Father, as we are taught to do, it is not by courtesy or a figure of speech ; it is a statement of a positive fact. It follows as a necessary consequence that the intellectual faculties, which are the masculine qualities of man's nature, and the affections, which are the feminine qualities of his nature, were derived from the Lord.

These factors of the human mind, which in general terms we call love and wisdom, or goodness and truth, must be united in every human being. Love alone does not constitute a human being, neither does truth alone. The two qualities or factors must be united. Love has its form and means of action from truth, and truth has all its power from love. They must be conjoined—married—before either of these two essential elements of the human mind can act. This union is not an artificial one. It is like that of substance and form.   Each becomes the other, and together they make one.

Here, then, we find the origin of marriage.   It is derived from the Lord.   It has its highest and perfect form in Him, for in Him love and wisdom are one.   We do not mean by this that they are the same.   His wisdom is the adequate and perfect form of His love, and His love finds full and adequate expression and embodiment in His wisdom.   There is no excess of the one over the other, as there is in human minds.   As they go forth in the creation they become embodied in spiritual and material forms, distinct from one another, each one embodying the same essential elements, but in different proportions, and each seeking the other and drawn to the other by a power derived from their common origin.   This power we call attraction, which literally means "drawing to."   The particles of matter have an affinity for one another, and they draw those of a homogeneous nature to themselves and combine, are joined together, or are married, and form other bodies.   Gases marry and become liquids and solids, as water and precious stones.   The earth draws all things to herself. The sun draws all planets to his fiery bosom. There is, moreover, throughout creation, in its largest and least forms, a duality. There is everywhere the passive and the active ; objects are adapted for each other and find their use in union with each other. Everywhere they possess more or less perfectly the qualities of masculine and feminine, male and female, and present an image of marriage.

This general principle running through all, separating all, combining all, gives unity in infinite variety. The union between man and woman, which we call marriage, is only an eminent instance of the universal marriage by which each is bound to all, and all to the Lord. Marriage, therefore, has its origin in the Lord, and its highest and universal form in the union between love and wisdom, or good and truth. Marriage originates, derivatively, in the inmost degrees and principles of man's spirit ; in the germs and beginnings of his nature as a human being. God created man male and female. God joined man and woman together as He joined heat and light, affection and thought, heart and lungs, love and wisdom. Marriage has its origin, therefore, in God; its highest, inmost, fullest created form and manifestation in man and woman.

Such being the origin of marriage, we proceed to the second question we are to consider, which is, the nature of marriage. This is necessarily involved in its origin. But the subject is so large and important, and one which is so little understood, that it will richly repay special consideration.

As marriage has its human origin in the first principles and most interior forms of man's nature, it consists essentially in the union of two minds or souls. The human spirit is the subject and theatre of its operation. It is, therefore, spiritual in its nature. It is not in itself a civil or legal contract; it is not effected by ecclesiastical sanction. It is as impossible for the state or the church to marry a man and a woman, in the essential meaning of the word, as it would be to join light and heat, or make two material substances combine which had no affinity for each other. The state may throw restraints around marriage; it may prescribe legal forms and conditions for its natural and visible consummation ; it may protect and conserve it by the sanctions of its authority, as it is its right and duty to do ; but it can neither unite nor separate human souls. The church may give its sanction, and consecrate its consummation by solemn ceremonies; it may instruct the people in its nature and use, and the proper steps that lead to it; but here its mission and power end. It cannot touch the interior and invisible bonds that bind soul to soul, either to confirm or dissolve them. God alone can join human souls together, and of the twain make one.

This fact, that real marriage can be effected only by Him who created man male and female, will appear more clearly, if possible, when we consider the nature of that power that conjoins the man and woman and of the two makes one. The power which draws man and woman to each other, and binds them together, and unites their souls, is love, which is spiritual attraction, and, like the attraction between material bodies, it operates in interior ways. Love effects and consecrates the real marriage. The degree and nature of the love determine the degree and nature of the marriage and the plane of man's nature in which it is effected. This is an essential truth, and has a most important bearing upon the whole subject. It is impossible to understand the essential nature of marriage without some knowledge of the fact that there are distinct planes or degrees of the human mind, each of which has its distinct faculties and qualities. It is from ignorance of this fact that the church has believed and taught that sex is merely a physical distinction and marriage a temporary relation whose bonds are dissolved by the dissolution of the material body. When it is nothing but a civil contract for worldly and natural considerations, the dissolution of the material body will sever all its bonds, as it does every bargain and civil bond. But if the marriage is a union of souls, nothing but the destruction of the soul itself can sunder the ties which unite them.

The doctrines of the New Church, in which the organization of man's spirit is disclosed and set forth in the most specific, rational, and logical forms, and in the fullest manner, all derived from the Word of God, teach that man as to his spirit is a threefold being. Marriage can be effected on either of these planes, and its nature will depend entirely upon the degree of life in which the husband and wife are united. If they come together for merely natural, worldly, and selfish motives, because of wealth and social position, or physical beauty, or natural possessions, the union is a marriage only in name. It is more properly a bargain, a copartnership between the man and woman by which they agree to live together as husband and wife, for the attainment and possession of some natural good. No spiritual principle enters into it ; no spiritual affection is awakened by it. There is no union of souls. There is no giving and receiving of personal life. It is not a real marriage. Husband and wife are not joined together interiorly by God. It is an agreement, a copartnership to secure a personal good, rather than a union of hearts by which each becomes the other's.

Such a partnership between a man and woman may result in much natural happiness. The husband and wife have common interests, which can be promoted by mutual and united effort.

The Sanctity of Marriage

There is a constant interchange of thought and
service. They become accustomed to each
other's ways and peculiarities of thought and
character, and learn to adapt themselves to each
other. Custom grows into habit. They have
common joys, common duties, and common sorrows, and they become necessary to each other.
Probably the great majority of marriages are of
this nature. They relate only to this life and
this world. Husband and wife are bound together only by natural affection, and this affection is not primarily the love of each other, but
of some common good. It is not the love of
rendering the other a service, but of receiving
service from the other. The inspiration of the
marriage is love of self rather than love of the
Lord and the neighbor, and the relation does not
rise above the level of a business partnership.
It is often attended by some measure of outward success, but sometimes with miserable failure ; and at the best it is hollow and without
interior blessing.

When we rise to the spiritual plane of our
nature, we come into the presence of faculties

where a genuine marriage is possible. Here we find the love of what is good and true as the essential characteristic of the affections and the motive of all action. It is the love of others for what they are, rather than for what they possess. It is primarily the love of goodness and truth. The splendor of truth attracts more than the brilliance of the eye; the grace of a well-ordered intelligence is prized above a pleasing manner; the fresh beauty of innocence is more charming than the clearest and fairest complexion; a true, steadfast, and pure affection is more precious than any or all merely natural gifts and possessions. Respect and honor and worship combine in pure and unselfish affection. There is true nobility in it. It equally dignifies and ennobles the one who gives and the one who receives it. When a man finds a woman worthy of such love, and capable of receiving, appreciating, and reciprocating it, when a woman finds a man capable of exercising it, they have secured all the conditions for a genuine marriage. They are united by bonds which neither time nor space nor material conditions nor death nor life can sever.

The bonds are substantial, indissoluble, and will continue to draw them into closer and more blissful union forever. Each loves the other for what the other is and can receive ; each desires to give to the other of his or her own, to become the other's own. Thus, by mutual giving and receiving, they are joined together and become one. This is the nature of true, spiritual marriage.

And if we rise to the highest plane of human life and the most interior faculties of the soul, we find that man and woman attain their most intimate and holiest union as they join in love and service of the Lord. This is the highest marriage, and it becomes pure and blessed as that love and service are so.

The ground of marriage consists in the fact that man and woman are created complements of each other ; they are so made that each needs and loves the qualities possessed by the other. The woman loves intelligence in the man. She is charmed with his ability to discover the secret laws of nature and apply its forces to human use. This ability and his strength in overcoming the antagonism of men in the arena of life are a staff to lean upon, a shield to protect, and the magician's wand to compel the elements into her service and provide her with the means of happiness. All the qualities of the masculine nature are the mates and complements of her affections. They round out and complete her own being.

And the man loves the woman for her beauty of form and grace of manner, for her pliancy and gentleness. He loves her for her strength, because it is of a different nature from his own ; it is the strength of love. He delights to be overcome and yield to that. It matches his power of intellect and proves her his equal, though she uses different weapons and wields them with a skill impossible to him. Her soft and gentle hand is a match for his hard and muscular one. She conquers by winning, he by force of muscle and brain. He storms the citadel ; she gains possession of it by secret and charming ways which make it pleasant to surrender. Defeat under these conditions is better than victory,—or rather, there is no defeat. Both surrender and both are victorious. Both attain what they desire. The woman gives beauty and grace to the man's strength, and

he gives power and substantial form to her affections. Faculty is wedded to faculty, and each gives
and receives what the other needs. Both natures
are enriched and perfected by the exchange.
Both gain and neither loses.

In a true marriage there is this remarkable
result, which is possible only in the spiritual plane
of the creation. The twain become one not by
the merging and absorption of one into the other
and the loss of personal identity, as two drops of
water melt into one. Each becomes the other,
but remains more distinctly herself or himself.
The husband is not changed into a woman, nor
the wife into a man. On the contrary, the wife
becomes more distinctly feminine in all her faculties, and the husband more distinctly masculine.
The unity which marriage effects is not the unity
of sameness, but of harmony in variety. The
peculiar qualities and the forms of sex are more
clearly revealed and sharply defined. Each partner comes into greater freedom of thought because
the intellectual faculties of both husband and wife
are perfected. They come into greater freedom ;
and as they go on into the eternal future, and

each one becomes enlarged and perfected by the mutual interchange of thought and love, the wife will become more distinctly and beautifully and charmingly feminine, and the husband will become more nobly and grandly masculine, and both will come into more intimate and distinct and blissful union.

Such, as we understand it, and as the New Church teaches, is the origin and nature of marriage. It is the union of one man and one woman in the bonds of a pure and holy love derived from the Lord and descending through heaven from Him.

Such being its nature, it follows as a necessary consequence that there can be no human relation so sacred as this. It contains in itself, in its essential nature, and in the manifold legitimate forms of its manifestation and use, all that is orderly, lovely, pure, and holy. It is a lower and special form of the union of the Lord with the individual soul and with the church, which He calls His bride and wife. It is the most intimate, the most perfect and blissful relation which one human being can hold to another. It is implanted in the constitution of man's nature and woman's nature ; it is a union to which they are predestined by the Divine love and wisdom, and by every faculty of their constitution and principle of their being. It is the union of homogeneous natures by which each finds the complement of itself and attains its own perfection.

Such being the high and sacred nature of real, genuine marriage, it follows as a necessary consequence that anything which tends to hinder its consummation is a loss ; that any violation of its sanctities is a most deadly sin, and that every truth which throws light upon its true nature, and helps man and woman to find the complement of their souls, is the most precious gift that man or God can bestow upon them.

II.

HOW TRUE MARRIAGES ARE FORMED.

"What . . . God hath joined together."—MARK x. 9.

THE Lord creates man in pairs, and these pairs are specifically related, like the heart and lungs. Each part is made for one other, and for no other but that one. It will not fit any other; it cannot unite perfectly with any other. This specific adaptation is as perfect in human beings as it is in the components of any material substance. The Divine wisdom is not limited to a general arrangement of the substances and forces in the creation. It operates in the least things and in the most specific manner. The Lord is faithful in that which is least, and in this way He becomes faithful in much. What a defect and defeat of the creation it would be if it were left to chance and accident whether an animal or a child was born without a heart or lungs, or with half a brain, or with only one hand or foot! It would be just as great a defect in the Divine methods if it were left to chance to provide the complement to every human being's nature which he needs to gain the happiness for which he was created.

A true marriage, which consists in the union of souls, can take place only between those souls that were made for each other. Only those can unite. There may be what is called marriage between a man and woman of the most opposite nature. That is a merely external and legal union. But a real marriage goes deeper. It is not determined by circumstance ; it is not formed by merely natural and worldly means. In such legal connections the man and the woman—we can call them husband and wife only by common courtesy and common usage—meet on the material and merely natural plane of life. Their thoughts and affections are limited to this world and to this life. They may get along comfortably, be of great assistance to each other, and enjoy much of natural life, and yet have no communion of spiritual and human affection and thought.

But man is a spiritual being. He is destined by every faculty of his nature to find his home and the means of his happiness in the spiritual world. The longest life in this world, compared with his life in the spiritual world, is as a moment to eternal years. It is as the acorn which lies in the ground for a few months, compared with the oak which lives for centuries. Our life in the material world is the acorn ; our life in the spiritual world is the undying oak. The Lord provides for the organization of man's spiritual nature and its perpetual development. He bends every event and natural circumstance to man's permanent and highest good. He provides for it in the creation of human pairs and in their preparation for union. They may be separated by time and space and circumstance, and even by worlds. They may never meet in this world, and still the preparation may be going on for the eternal union of natures destined to be joined together by God.

If this fact were known and understood, it would have a most important influence on all our thoughts and purposes with regard to marriage in this world. We should regard it as the most important relation that exists between one human being and another. It would enter into and control all our purposes and the whole conduct of life. Young men and women would be instructed in the nature and importance of this relation, and how to prepare themselves for it. While it is true that human beings are created in pairs, and every one has a specific nature and original endowment of faculties for union with a corresponding nature, this creation is not completed, and, as it were, stereotyped and unchangeably fixed by one act of creative power. The work is continually going on. It is true that the first step enters into all the subsequent ones and modifies them. But the original endowment is also modified by all the influences and means that are active in its development. Human freedom enters as a large factor in the result. A human being is not made as the artist moulds an image in the soft and passive clay, or cuts it in marble. Man himself co-operates with the Lord in his creation. The Lord says to every human being, "Let us make man." Every man and woman, therefore, co-operates with the Lord in determining the final result. What each one be-

comes, without any knowledge of the unknown
being who is the complement of his or her
. nature, is determining who that being shall be.
Every one is becoming the complement of some
other being by the character formed. The knowledge gained, the affections cherished, the habits
confirmed, the character organized, are all elements which must enter into, modify, and determine the result.

Common observation and universal experience
testify to this fact. Why is there a reciprocal
attraction between one young man and one
young woman rather than between others? Is
it not because there are qualities of heart, some
peculiarities of manner, some graces of form and
speech, of look and act, that are specially pleasing?
But these are mostly the result of culture in its
largest sense. The whole life in all its acts and
apparently trivial circumstances has contributed
to the result. What the boy and girl are doing
in early childhood and youth, the innocent affections they exercise which give to the morning of
life the charm that fragrance and tender beauty
give to the flower, the education of circumstance

and relation, and the little unnoticed daily acts as well as the formal instruction, give quality to the affections, color and form to the intellect, tone to speech, and grace, or the want of it, to manner; all combine to determine those special and peculiar qualities that constitute individuality and prepare for union with one person rather than another. It is in the nature of things, therefore, that boys and girls and men and women are determining, by the characters they form, to whom they are to be joined in eternal union. They are to be matched and mated. They are to find their counterpart, the complement of their form and nature. But what that counterpart will be must be determined by what each one is and becomes.

It necessarily follows from this that in an important sense every man and woman has the power of determining, and is determining, who the real partner shall be. The responsibility of choice is committed to each one. The man may ask, Where am I to find my wife? The woman may ask, Where am I to find my husband? The answer must be, Look within your own mind and

see what manner of man or woman you are.
Who will fit you? That must be determined by
what you are. God cannot join incongruous
natures together, much less those of opposite
and hostile character. The pure and the vile are
not homogeneous; evil is not the complement
of good, virtue of vice. They are as opposite as
heat and cold, light and darkness. God cannot
join them together. He can join those natures
only which are the complements of each other.

True marriages are formed, and can be formed,
only by the cultivation of those faculties which
can be united. The man must cultivate and develop those faculties that are distinctly masculine
in form and quality. The woman must cherish
and perfect those qualities of heart and intellect
that are distinctly feminine. The union of the
masculine and feminine mind is not the conjunction of the same mental qualities. It is not the
direct union of heart with heart, or thought with
thought, as is often supposed. It is the union of
the will of the one with the understanding of the
other, of affection with thought, and thought with
affection. The wife does not love the husband

28

because he possesses the same qualities of brain and heart that she does. She has no desire to marry herself. She does not want a wife, but a husband. The husband does not love the wife for masculine qualities, but for womanly ones. He does not want a man for a wife. Men of great intellectual powers are often devotedly attached to wives who are quite their opposites in this respect. The man has an intellect already. It is not a library, or a dictionary, or a geological cabinet he needs. He wants intelligence, it is true, but not in its cold and sharp forms. He seeks it clothed in the garments of feminine beauty and bathed in the warm light of love. He is not attracted by the dry bones of truth; he seeks it clothed with living flesh and rounded into graceful feminine forms. On the other hand, the woman is not charmed by weak and blind affection. She desires love, but she prizes it in the power and glorious form of truth. She loves wisdom, but wisdom is love directed by truth to a noble purpose. This is a universal law of the Divine order, which is beautifully exemplified in chemical affinities and in the numberless combinations of matter in the creation of material objects. Affinity is not due to sameness, identity, but to those qualities which mutually accommodate and adapt substances to one another, and enable them by their union to form a more excellent whole.

Every woman is preparing herself for marriage by the disposition and qualities of head and heart she is cherishing. This is true not only in general but in particular. Every affection must have its corresponding truth, which is the form and measure of it ; the affection itself determines with what truth it shall be joined. If we have one of the elements of a substance we desire to form, we must obtain the other ; and what the other will be must be determined by the one we possess. If we desire to form water and have hydrogen, any gas will not answer; we must have oxygen; we must have the element that will combine with the one we possess. The one we possess then determines the one we must procure. According to the same principle, what a man or woman becomes by heredity, by education, and by culture in its widest and most specific sense, determines who the corresponding partner shall be. To every woman, in a large degree, therefore, is given the choice of her husband, and to every man the choice of his wife, and every one is choosing by the character he or she is forming. Each one is becoming the measure of the other; each one is developing the special qualities that must find a correspondent. Each one is making preparation for marriage, and determining who the partner shall be, by every affection exercised, by every thought indulged and every deed done. Chance, or circumstance, or casual meeting have no control over the final result. Beings that are the complements of one another cannot be kept apart. No obstacles of time, or place, or circumstance can prevent the union of those whom God has destined for each other. They may never meet in this world, but congenial souls cannot fail to find each other when all natural obstructions are removed. The force that draws them together pervades the spiritual universe, touches every soul in the innumerable multitude, as the magnet finds the least atom of iron and separates it from every other substance. Those whom God has destined for each other cannot be kept asunder.

This certainty of result in the operation of the Divine laws, and the agency which we have in the result, bring the whole question home to each one of us personally, and lay upon us the responsibility and necessity of choice, because our free choice in the formation of our own characters is a part of the Divine plan. It is our share in the preparation that concerns us, and the knowledge that it is a most important factor in determining the result must have great influence with us in the ordering of our lives. If we were called together, knowing that whatever we brought was to be matched in quality and quantity and to become ours ; if the material of our garments would determine the materials of which all future garments were to be made ; if the ornaments we wore, or the metal of our money would be what we should forever possess, should we come in coarse and faded attire ? Should we adorn ourselves with tinsel and glass when we could put on gold and diamonds ? Should we fill our purses with coppers and nickels instead of silver and gold ?

How True Marriages are Formed

There is not a boy or a girl, a man or a woman, who would be guilty of such folly. Let us not, then, be guilty of the infinitely greater folly of being indifferent to what we become, because that will determine the character of him or her who is to be our other self, with whom we are to become indissolubly one.

In view of this law of the Divine order, from which it is as impossible to escape as from the power of attraction, let us consider some of the special means by which we are to determine the character of husband or wife.

As marriage is the destiny of every man and woman, and the means which the Lord has provided for our happiness, we should look forward to it as the most desirable, the most intimate and sacred relation in life. Parents should instruct their children in the principles of its nature, and as far as possible provide the means for a correct knowledge of its importance. Many do labor diligently to provide the means for its natural wants and comforts. But when its true nature is understood and in some degree appreciated, they will be still more solicitous and diligent in pro-

3   33

viding the means for a more adequate appreciation of its spiritual importance, and for meeting its responsibilities and wisely performing its duties. Parents will not accomplish this by trying to find a suitable match, as judged by natural standards, but by training up their sons and daughters to become worthy of pure and noble partners.

In due time young people should diligently and faithfully begin to prepare themselves for this union. This should not be done in the silly and ruinous way that is so common, by thinking of this one or that, magnifying the importance of wealth and station and material conditions, but by making themselves worthy to mate the worthy, knowing that what they themselves are determines who are to be the complements of their being.

The true effort to prepare for marriage leads to the shunning of every evil that would taint the purity of marriage, and every error that would tend to disturb its harmony. This will be a most powerful motive in regulating the conduct of life. The young man and the young woman will say, If I am the measure of what I desire in husband or wife, I must raise the standard of excellence as high as possible. If I desire an unselfish companion through the eternal years, I must myself be unselfish. I must be pure if I would be linked to purity. I must be kind if I am to expect kindness, truthful if I am to wed the truth, faithful to every trust if I desire fidelity in my other self. I must shun in myself every imperfection that could lessen my respect for husband or wife and tend to separate us.

This would lead to the cultivation of those amiable traits of character which prevent friction and give a charm to the most intimate human relations. It would be a powerful and constantly operating motive to form habits and acquire graces and accomplishments that would break the monotony and relieve the drudgery of constant labor, and make the daily contacts in the journey of life a pleasure rather than a weariness and an annoyance. It would stimulate to industry, to a wise economy, and to wisdom in the conduct of affairs. It would quicken the desire to become intelligent and to cultivate all the qualities that would grace and make rich in promise and experience the union of two natures in one mind.

It is too often the case in marriage that the husband expects the wife to yield entirely to his wishes, and the wife cherishes the vain hope that the husband will yield even to her whims and caprices. These expectations furnish the conditions for inevitable disappointment and division. The true grounds of union are directly the reverse. The young woman should cultivate a love of what is right, true, and wise, and should seek for these qualities in the husband, that it may be a delight to yield to him and be guided by him as their embodiment. The young man should cherish the love of what is good and true, and seek the embodiment of this love in his wife. So far as he succeeds he will love to yield to the power of her love and to be led by her affection. In this state each one desires to be the other's, each one desires to give and to receive, and the result is harmony of thought and affection and unity of life. The husband and wife cherish a sacred regard for the rights and happiness of each other. There is no question who shall yield. They both yield. There is no conflict to decide who shall govern. They govern conjointly. There is no question who is the greatest and wisest and best. Each one thinks the other is the greatest, the wisest, and the best. The result is freedom, harmony, and union.

It may be said that there are no such perfect men and women. This may be so; but it cannot be denied that this excellence of character is what every one should aspire to and strive to attain. Every woman should aim to become a perfect woman, and every man should aim to become a perfect man. This is the goal all should seek; and when we have a true idea of what human perfection is, it is not so difficult of attainment as is generally supposed. Perfection consists in doing the best we can, according to the measure of our knowledge and ability. An infant may be perfect as an infant in all its ignorance and helplessness. Boys and girls can be perfect according to their ability. A woman can be a perfect daughter, sister, wife, mother; and she is perfect in all these relations when she faithfully performs all her duties according to her best knowledge and ability. The Lord makes the ability of every one the standard of perfection for him, and judges him by that. He gives the same commendation of "good and faithful servant" to the one who has five pounds that He does to the one who has ten. Perfection is a relative attainment for a human being. The only absolutely perfect Being is the Lord. It is towards that perfection that we should move. Our happiness will not consist in attaining it, but in striving to be perfect as our Father in heaven in perfect ; and every step we take towards Him will be a perfect step if taken according to the best of our knowledge and ability.

Marriage, like regeneration, or the attainment of any excellence, is a gradual process. The preparation for it begins in time, and some steps in its accomplishment may be taken in this world, but it never can be completed here. Indeed, there is no point in the degree and perfection of the union between two homogeneous natures that will not be passed. A true marriage is not only an eternal union, but it is a continually increasing union. The ceremony that legalizes or consecrates the marriage is only an incident in the real union. It is an important incident, and should be reverently regarded. It is a landmark in the progress of marriage, but it is not the beginning or the end of it. It gives to it the sanction of law, and the freedom of personal intimacy, which is most favorable to real union of thought and affection.

The genuine marriage is formed by the interchange of intelligence and affection in daily life. The will and understanding of husband and wife meet and become conjoined in the common duties and pleasures of social, domestic, and personal life. Thought is received and adopted by affection, and affection by thought. The kind look, the true word, the helping hand, the loving tone, the gentle caress, the quick sympathy, and the innumerable and unconscious ways in which affection expresses itself are flying from will to understanding, and from understanding to will, and weaving the two natures into one web. By these mutual and constant contacts the bonds of affection are forming and gaining strength, and the power of mutual attraction is constantly increasing and drawing soul closer to soul.

It is true that there are many obstacles in the nature of both husband and wife to this interior and genuine marriage. Great difficulties must be met and overcome. Much must be surrendered that is very dear and hard to relinquish. There is immense significance in the words, "Therefore shall a man leave his father and his mother, and shall cleave unto his wife." The father and mother that both husband and wife must leave before they become one flesh, one life, are the supreme love of self and the world, and there is no treasure so precious to the natural mind as this love. It is indeed the life that we must all lay down before we can become one with the Lord and each other. It will cost many a struggle and much keen anguish, and sometimes despair.

The relations of husband and wife are peculiarly adapted to effect this surrender of each to the other. The intercourse and reciprocal services of daily life constantly call for the suppression of self and for mutual service in little things which are not too great for our strength. So we give up one point after another, and every position of self abandoned is seized by a true love. The surrender and the victory are mutual. The husband gets more than he gives ; the wife gains more than she loses. Each one gets a nobler and a purer self. Each one gains a larger power over the other, and becomes more distinctly and consciously free. This process of giving and receiving, of surrender and victory, will go on until all the obstacles of union are removed and free play can be given to every affection, to seek and find its corresponding self.

In all these trials and temptations God is joining husband and wife together. The fine filaments of thought spun, as it were, from their life, like the fibres with which the silk-worm weaves its cocoon, are twisted into one thread which becomes a living bond binding each to each, and forming the line along which the messages of mutual affection constantly pass and repass. All that is not homogeneous to both is being gradually displaced, and in each a new nature, a new self, is forming, which is the image of the other, different but corresponding. The wife becomes the image of the husband, but in feminine forms. The husband becomes the likeness of the wife, but in masculine lines, as a daughter resembles her father and a son his mother. The nature of each is modified and completed by the other, but in the process of assimilation the wife becomes more distinctly and beautifully feminine, and the husband more distinctly and nobly masculine. There is no merging of one nature with another by which each loses some distinctive quality, as two drops of water melt into one. This would destroy all individuality and all ground of affection and possibility of marriage. The lines which distinguish husband and wife are more firmly drawn. The more closely they are united, the more distinct the union.

Some conditions of life seem to be more favorable for the formation of this union than others. But this we cannot know. There is no condition wholly incompatible with it. Where husband and wife, by natural law, possess such incompatible natures that no real union between them is possible, still the one or the other or both may be exercising those qualities which will prepare for a true marriage. The wife may be developing the purest and noblest feminine qualities, with a patience, fidelity, and heroism, under stress of opposition and desertion, which will fit her for a corresponding noble nature. The same may be true of the husband. Those who are truly married in heart and soul may be separated by time and space or the dissolution of the material body, and still be cherishing those affections and cultivating that love and wisdom in the conduct of their lives which will, at the proper time, and in the orderly ways which the Lord will provide, bring them into conscious and blissful union with those who possess corresponding natures. We come, therefore, to this conclusion : that every woman prepares herself for a true marriage by cultivating and becoming the embodiment and form of womanly dispositions and qualities of mind and heart ; that every man prepares himself for a true marriage by becoming a pure, true, and noble man, and in this way becoming worthy of a corresponding pure, true, and noble woman. Through whatever phases of life they may pass, and whatever natural unions they may form, every one will be joined by God with the one who is his or her measure. And those whom God joins together can never be put asunder, but will continue forever to come into a more blissful union. The process of marriage will never cease.

III.

THE MINISTRY OF MARRIAGE IN REGENERATION.

"*From the beginning of the creation God made them male and female.*

"*For this cause shall a man leave his father and mother, and cleave to his wife;*

"*And they twain shall be one flesh: so then they are no more twain, but one flesh.*"—MARK x. 6-8.

MARRIAGE is the most sacred and intimate relation that can exist between human beings. Man was created male and female, that each one might find some object out of himself to love, and that by reciprocal affection the spiritual natures of both man and woman might become enlarged in their capacities for the reception of the Divine life, and, by mutual help, that they might become one. And in the Golden Age of humanity they did become one by a process of orderly and harmonious development. As the distinctive nature of man and woman unfolded, each one put forth tendrils of thought and affection that were clasped

45

by the other; and while the man became more
distinctly masculine and the woman more distinctly feminine, they grew together into a more
indissoluble and perfect unity. Each one helped
the other to a more distinct personality; and the
currents of their lives, having their source in the
fountain of the Lord's life, flowed into each other,
and flowed on together in unfailing and ever
deepening streams. The spiritual degrees of
mind of those innocent men and women flowed
down into all human relations, bringing the life
and the light of heaven into all their natural
thoughts and affections, into all their words and
deeds. The spiritual degrees of mind were harmo-
niously developed. They grew into each other's
likeness and into the likeness of the Lord.

When man fell from a spiritual to a merely
natural life, the whole order of his nature became
inverted; the spiritual planes of his nature became
divorced from the natural, and having no basis
and no means of development, they became as
dead, and man began to live wholly for himself.
His thoughts and affections centred in himself.
His regard for others was measured by what he

could make them do for him. Man and woman
became spiritually divorced from each other by
everything that was false and evil in their natures.
But while there were many causes that tended to
drive them asunder, there were many still remaining that drew them together. Before the fall
there was not a principle or a faculty, from the
inmost to the outmost of the masculine or feminine being, which did not lead each to seek the
other. By the death of the spiritual life the
highest and most powerful sources of this conjoining power were cut off, and many of the
merely natural tendencies to union were perverted.
But many external links binding man and woman
together still remained. Man and woman in every
age and every state have been drawn towards
each other; and while there has been much to
hinder and repel, they have still found and must
ever find mutual help in bearing life's burdens, in
performing its labors and in overcoming the obstacles to their regeneration, and in regaining the
interior union and perfection of the state from
which they fell. I ask your attention to a statement of some of the ways in which marriage, even

in the low and imperfect forms in which it now exists, assists the husband and wife in putting away their natural evils and falsities, and tends to the development of a genuine spiritual life.

The principal obstacles to man's regeneration are the love of self and of the world. Marriage is the great and most perfect school for learning and practising self-denial, and the exercise of those spiritual affections which constitute a spiritual life ; and this is the special aspect in which I propose to present the subject.

The woman was created that she might convert the love of the man for himself into his love for her. The end of marriage, therefore, so far as it relates to spiritual culture and regeneration, is the prevention of self-love, or its subjugation. It effects this end in various ways, and is one of the most beautiful examples of the manner in which the Lord provides for man in every state, and employs the same means to develop his spiritual nature, to restrain him from going farther astray, and to bring him back to unity with the Divine life and to harmony with the life of his fellowmen.

The Ministry of Marriage

In the present state of humanity it is hardly possible that there will not be many obstacles to a complete spiritual union between husband and wife. Persons who have been educated in different families and in circumstances widely unlike must have acquired different habits and tastes; must view many questions in various if not opposite aspects, and there must be much that has become a second nature, to hold in abeyance, to change, and to surrender, before the unity of interior life can be established in external act. The first jar that disturbs the harmony of the union between husband and wife often arises from these diversities of taste and habit. Self-love delights to have its own way. It always feels that it ought to be gratified even when it does not insist upon it. If it keeps silent, a little is gained, for when self-assertion is restrained in the least, a step is taken in the right direction. If it yields from regard to another, it enters upon the most difficult work of regeneration.

The first state of married life is very favorable to the beginning of this work. The young husband and wife invest each other with many ideal perfections. The natural imagination is active, and throws a halo of light over every beloved object. It magnifies virtues and overlooks defects and clothes all things with its own hues. This ideal life is the blossoming of those faculties which are to ripen into fruit ; the sweet prophecy of joys which may spring up all along the pathway of life, as the essential character is developed, growing brighter and purer as the spiritual and heavenly planes of the mind become unfolded. Those who mistake the flowers for the fruit are no doubt disappointed when they fade and fall. But this very illusion calls off the attention from real difficulties and disguises habits of thought and life, until objects of common interest in the various household arrangements and in the many plans for the future become absorbing. Thus, as one bond weakens others become stronger, and the fibres are forming which are to be woven into the web of their mutual life, and bind husband and wife into one. We may suffer the bright hopes and expectations, which shot up wild and disorderly in our young imaginations, to live about our homes, and, without robbing them

of their savor and bright hues, may sort each
with its kind, and hedge them round with the
binding growth of family attachments. Thus
even in the beginning the conditions are most
favorable to meet the exact wants and difficulties
of married life. If marriage were invested with
no hues of fancy, if it were not made roseate
and glorious with hopes issuing from the opening
fountain of life, if nothing but the hard and un-
relenting facts appeared, we might shrink from
this contact, and fail to obtain the rich blessings
they are the rough instrument of conveying.
The same law operates in every relation and duty
of life. We never should gain the goal we value
above all price, if we saw from the beginning all
the difficulties which lie in the way.

But when the dissimilar habits and contrarieties
of taste and opposite views begin to appear
through the dissolving mists of youthful fancy, a
multitude of mutual hopes and mutual fears have
been formed ; there are many pleasant memories
whose influence still lingers like the fragrance
of flowers ; there are a multitude of events
constantly occurring in which the husband and

wife have a mutual interest. If they look
to the future, they cannot fail to see that their
happiness depends upon their mutual forbear-
ance and helpfulness, and a most powerful
motive is presented to yield their own predilec-
tions and to conform to the habits and tastes
of each other. If they have any wisdom they
will yield to the necessity, and they will find
their happiness in it.

When the love of husband and wife for each
other is genuine and unselfish, this renunciation
of self for the sake of the other will be spontaneous and delightful. Self will be forgotten in
the desire to live solely for another, and the
greater the external contrariety of taste and
habit the better the opportunity to show the
depth and strength of affection. When this is
the case the beginning of regeneration becomes
pleasant even, and we become initiated into the
great and most important work of our lives without pain and conflict, and even by processes of
delight. The husband and wife begin to render
to each other the service for which they were
created and destined. They are a help to each

other in becoming all that their most glowing
fancies ever conceived, and ineffably more.

But this is only the beginning. We have all
much more to put away than diversities of taste,
or dissimilar habits, or opposite opinions on mat-
ters of natural interest. A man or woman of
even temper and established principles may meet
these difficulties with composure, may yield without much apparent self-sacrifice and without any
humiliation. But no persons can hold such intimate relations as husband and wife long, without
penetrating beneath the surface and unveiling the
secret springs of life. The mask we have worn,
unconsciously to ourselves perhaps, will be removed, and our little weaknesses which, it may
be, we cherish more than anything else, will be
exposed ; or the secret and selfish springs of
action which constitute our inmost life are dis-
covered by the sharp eyes of vigilant love. That
is a discovery at which self-love may well trem-
ble. There is just cause to fear that we who
have been almost worshipped as a superior being
shall fall from our high position, and there is no
more certain or terrible cross for self-love than

this. And when we find, as we shall often and always find when there is any real love for each other, that such discoveries are regarded with that beautiful charity which thinketh no evil and invests the objects of its affection with its own robe of whiteness, we shall be humbled and the force of our own selfishness will be weakened. Our evils appear more hateful to us than ever before. We shall keep a more vigilant watch over our hearts and lips, and strive more earnestly to be all that innocent and unsuspecting affection has ever imagined us to be.

There is another principle of our nature which tends to repress and prevent any selfish act, and that is fear; not the fear that we may be injured, but that we may injure and alienate affection. This fear must ever attend any profound and delicate regard for others. We are too ignorant of ourselves and others ; we are continually liable to misapprehension. We know how impossible it is for us to express ourselves clearly, and how prone we are to mistake a casual outburst of feeling for a settled principle of character; and the more fully we are aware of these defects in

ourselves the more carefully we shall guard
against putting a wrong construction upon the
words or actions of others. We shall fear to do
them wrong, and this will lead us to strive to give
them no occasion to distrust us. It will lead us
to repress and put away everything in our conduct
and in our thoughts and affections even, that will
cause them a moment's pain. This holy fear
acts as a constant watch against selfishness, and
presents a powerful motive to repress and overcome it.

But the work of regeneration cannot be effected
suddenly. It is not the work of a day or a year,
but of a life. It is the putting off of our selfish,
evil nature, and the putting on of an unselfish and
good nature. And this can only be done little by
little. It cannot be effected in general without
descending into particulars. It is only those who
are faithful in the least that are faithful in much.
We must enter upon the work and carry it on,
thought by thought and act by act, in the most
common and least things. No condition can be
conceived more favorable to this necessity of the
work than married life. It is a daily and constant

life. It is not merely contact upon great occasions, but upon all points, at all times. The moments and the hours run as small filaments through the whole web of life. There is nothing that tries our temper and tests our resources like this. It is not difficult for the most unamiable and selfish to be agreeable for a time on set occasions. But no mask can withstand the attrition of daily and homely contact.

When there is no real love, this daily and constant attrition annoys and frets, and, like rust, eats away all the external beauty and polish of manner and formal intercourse. It forms the Liliputian cords which bind the strong man to the earth, and the poisoned arrows which nettle and sting the spirit to madness. But where natures are homogeneous, continual and intimate relations have the opposite effect. They serve to communicate the life of each to the other, and to give mutual help in the great work of spiritual culture. As the blood is propelled from the heart through the arteries to the inconceivably fine net-work of vessels which covers and penetrates the whole system, and there exerts its power to build up new tissue and to restore strength to the body, so the life that dwells in the heart of husband or wife must flow forth into innumerable uses and duties which cover and penetrate with their fine meshes the mind and soul of each. Here they come in contact. Here they give and receive mutual help. In the proper performance of these little things the wastes of life are repaired, and the great vital organs within are kept in vigorous and healthful activity. It is this faithfulness in these least things that renders us faithful in much. A pleasant look, a tone moulded with the winning harmonies of affection, a kind inquiry, a cheering word, the pleasant surprise of anticipated want, the cheerful surrender of some personal pleasure, a promptness to lend a helping hand to bear life's burdens and perform its duties,—these are the bonds which link souls together, and the medium through which they interchange their life.

These are also the most favorable opportunities for the subjugation of self. We can commence and carry on the work little by little, as all great and permanent changes are wrought. We are not disheartened at the greatness of the work. It is only a little surrender that must be made at any one time. Self-love and pride do not take the alarm, and thus we undermine and sap their strongest citadels. The work is not too great for our strength and goes imperceptibly on, until the force of our self-love is broken, and a natural affection gives place to a spiritual one. Spiritual affections and thoughts flow down into the natural and gain a lodgement in these orderly forms prepared for them, and begin to assume their proper office of restraining and guiding them.

It is also through these little channels, these common courtesies, these little unremembered acts, which, as has been well said, form the best portion of a good man's life,—it is through these sweet charities which we bring to the domestic altar that the interchange of life goes on. It is through these mediums that the electric fires in each heart play and fill the whole being with peaceful and interior delights. The husband and wife soon find in this reciprocal interchange of life that it is more blessed to give than to receive, and that giving does not impoverish but increases the store of love. They soon learn, by the faithful practice of these little duties, that their happi-

ness is on the side of unselfish affection, and lies
in the direction of self-surrender and along the
path of regenerate life.

This transfusion of the life of each into the life
of the other is the very order which our infinitely
wise Father has instituted by which to lift us up
from the low level of self and the world, and to
imbue us with His own Divine life. Each possesses
what the other needs. Man is cold, hard, rugged,
and obstinate. He needs some power to soften
and mould his nature to more beautiful forms.
He needs the warmth and ruddy life of a woman's
affection to blend with the cold whiteness of the
pure intellect, to warm it into a glowing activity.
Woman is quick, ardent, impulsive, liable to be
carried away by tides of natural feeling ; she needs
the strength, the firmness, and persistency of the
masculine intellect to keep all her graces well
balanced and give them harmonious play. Her
own loveliness is enhanced when the pure intellect
shines through the ruddy glow of her affections as
lilies and roses blend in her fair face. Thus the
beauty and strength of each is heightened, and
the whole nature in every respect is perfected by

what is given and received, and there is an actual advance in the regenerate life. Each one becomes more distinctly and fully an intelligent, conscious, and orderly recipient of the Divine life. They become more and more one flesh, and are approximating to the most noble human form, which is produced when two beings by means of marriage become one. The two do not become merged into one by sameness, by a loss of personality. Each one becomes more distinctly personal and gains in freedom. This union is not in any sense the losing of one's self, but of self-love. And this is the great work in regeneration.

But life is not made up wholly of these little daily duties. There are great events which constitute epochs in the history of married life, and are crises for good or evil. And these are necessary. The work of self-culture and regeneration is always a difficult one. Self-love and worldly affections operate as a constant hinderance. We are disposed to remain satisfied with low attainments, and we need something out of the ordinary course of every-day life to arrest our attention and to call into conscious activity new powers

and, it may be, new forms of selfish and worldly
affections, that we may combat and overcome them.
Married life furnishes us with many such occasions.

With the birth of parental love a new world is
opened in the father's and the mother's heart, a
world bright with many hopes and shadowed with
many fears. New fountains are unsealed in the
heart, fountains which may send forth both sweet
and bitter waters. A little child is always the
centre of attraction in the family, towards which
the affections, the hopes, and fears most powerfully
gravitate. Here is an object of mutual interest.
Here the affections and thoughts of parents meet
in pleasant interchange and perpetual play. Their
tenderness is called forth by the helpless innocent,
and their watchful care by its ever-recurring wants.
Their curiosity is excited by its rapidly unfolding
powers. They forget themselves. Here in this
little form is a great magnet which draws all
thoughts to it. Can we conceive any means better
adapted to draw out our affections for others and
to lead us to forget ourselves? It is true this
affection may be natural. But it is none the less

the gift of the Lord, and an actual derivation from
that love which joins all human beings together and
unites them with the Lord. It is the selfishness
of the natural mind that must be overcome. This
love is with many the beginning of a new life.
They begin to live for others in a fuller and more
unreserved manner. The true mother does not
think of herself. Her hopes and fears and affections are drawn out of and away from herself.
She lives for another, and her heart and head
never weary of loving and providing for her child.
The father's love may be less demonstrative, and
may manifest itself in different forms, but it is
none the less persistent and powerful for that.
He has a new motive to labor ; and while engaged
in his daily employment, his thoughts are busy
with the hopes or fears that centre in a beloved
child. In this way husband and wife are bound
together in the child, and the life of each is flowing
forth in a perennial stream of affection, thought,
and act to the other. Self and the world find
powerful rivals, and their power is weakened, if
not entirely broken.

And sooner or later most parents are called

upon to resign into the hands of Him who gave it, a child dearer perhaps than life itself. And this great sorrow may be the means of blessing. What parent can stand by the grave of a beloved child who has passed into the heavens, and not feel that much of the hardness and selfishness of his nature is dead and in the grave with the material body of his child? If parents have any idea of a life after this, they will follow the child in thought and affection to that world, and they will feel an interest in it which they never felt before. They have a treasure in heaven. Their eternal home lies beyond the veil of this life, and they must feel some drawings towards it. They resolve to live more for that world, and they make an effort to do it. Thus we find in our brightest joys and darkest sorrows something to crucify our selfishness and to bring into fuller activity those spiritual and heavenly affections which constitute our union with each other and our conjunction with the Lord.

It is not alone in the greatness of these joys and sorrows that we find help in the work of regeneration, but in the common interest of

The Sanctity of Marriage

husband and wife in those who are the objects
of their affections. There is a bond of mutual
sympathy running through every act. Every
shock brings married partners closer together;
every new joy is a new link in the golden chain
of affection; every common association is a fine
filament running through all the forms of their
life and weaving their natures into one. Thus in
all states there is a communication of the life of
each to the other.

In the beginning of married life, our hopes and
anticipations were serviceable in blinding us to‾
many of the hard realities and sacrifices of self,
alluring us on in the difficult work of self-renun-
ciation, by bright visions of ideal joys; so when
our earthly sun nears its setting, and life's pilgrim-
age draws towards its close, memory takes the
place of hope and helps to complete the work
which the glowing fancies of early manhood and
womanhood helped us to begin. There is no
sight on earth more touching than that of an aged
husband and wife who have been faithful and
devoted to each other during the long journey
that lies behind them. The fervors of youthful

passion have subsided; there may be less of the outward expression of affection, but there is a tenderness, a subdued, calm, and peaceful affection, a confidence born of many a struggle and many a triumph over self; a love seven times purified in the furnace of affliction. There is an innocence, not of the ignorance of infancy but of wisdom, shining soft and clear through the decaying walls of the body, like a bright day in autumn. As they look back along the pathway of life, they can see nothing in all its memories that does not draw them closer together and lead them to put away every remaining hinderance to their union in heart. In the far distant past they stood at the altar together and formally took upon themselves the vows which their own hearts had before made. From that mount of youthful hope, with all its brightness and strength about them, they descended into the plain of life's trials and duties and conflicts, and, as they follow their course in memory, many events of peculiar interest rise before them. There, in that dark valley, distrust threw its shadow over the brightness of early confidence; here selfishness tarnished the golden links of affection ; care began to write wrinkles upon the fair face, or sorrow dimmed the eyes, and they looked at each other through the mist of tears. Again they stood upon the mount of some noble affection, and the heaven above and within was clear and bright. There the husband or the wife faltered, weary and disheartened by the way, and gave occasion for a more absolute renunciation of self, and brought into fuller consciousness the tenderness of a manly heart, and the untiring constancy and persistent vigor of womanly strength. Now the Lord places a little child in their midst, and they forget themselves in their devotion to another, and in the glad surprises with which they watch the unfoldings of a new life. Again, they stand by an open grave and bury some of their evil and much of their natural life with the material garment of their child. And so the years roll on. They have shared many joys and many sorrows. They have made many mistakes. They have resigned much and they have gained much. But through these mutual labors and sorrows, hopes and joys, they have learned to forget and re-

nounce self. Their experiences have been so
many lessons in the knowledge and practice of
true charity. And as they review it they see still
more clearly the necessity and use of overcoming
every worldly and selfish affection. Whenever
they have renounced self and have shared each
other's joys or sorrows, they find without excep-
tion that the burden of sorrow and labor has
been lightened and the joy increased. The eternal law of the Divine order, that there is no true
life but in living for others, has been learned
and established as a principle of their own lives,
by long continued and most varied practice.

When marriage becomes a spiritual and
heavenly bond, it reunites the divided soul and
gives completeness to the masculine and feminine
nature. It gives delicacy to strength and strength
to delicacy. It breathes the warmth of love into
the coldness of the intellect, and tempers the
ardor of the passions with the cool light of the
understanding. It gives strength to the understanding and guidance to the will, in the mind of
both husband and wife. They grow into each
other's likeness by processes of delight; they

share and multiply each other's joys ; they divide
and bear each other's burdens. Each one
possesses all and becomes the other's self. God
joins them together. They twain become one,
and to the degree and extent of their unity they
are forms of heaven. Even in this life they have
a foretaste of its joys, and when they throw aside
the veil of clay, they will pass on and become the
mutual and reciprocal sharers of its endless and
ineffable and ever-increasing blessedness.

IV.

RESURRECTION AND MARRIAGE.

" *The same day came to him the Sadducees, which say that there is no resurrection, and asked him,*

"*Saying, Master, Moses said, If a man die, having no children, his brother shall marry his wife, and raise up seed unto his brother.*

" *Now there were with us seven brethren : and the first, when he had married a wife, deceased, and, having no issue, left his wife unto his brother :*

"*Likewise the second also, and the third, unto the seventh.*

"*And last of all the woman died also.*

" *Therefore in the resurrection, whose wife shall she be of the seven ? for they all had her.*

"*Jesus answered and said unto them, Ye do err, not knowing the scriptures, nor the power of God.*

" *For in the resurrection they neither marry, nor are given in marriage, but are as the angels of God in heaven.*

" *But as touching the resurrection of the dead, have ye not read that which was spoken unto you by God, saying,*

69

The Sanctity of Marriage

" I am the God of Abraham, and the God of Isaac, and the God of Jacob? God is not the God of the dead, but of the living.

*" And when the multitude heard this, they were aston-ished at his doctrine."—*MATTHEW xxii. 23–33.

THE Pharisees had been defeated in their attempt to entangle the Lord in His talk, and had been silenced by the unexpected wisdom of His reply. The Sadducees now come forward to try the same thing in their way. They attempt to entrap Him with a question from the Scriptures. They quote to Him Moses, and He answers them from Moses. The Sadducees were not sceptics; they were literalists. They believed in the letter of the Scriptures, and they rejected everything that was not plainly deducible from it. They rejected the traditions. They did not believe in a future life, because they declared that it was not taught in their Scriptures. They prided themselves on their knowledge of the Scriptures. They could quote texts to support every opinion they held. The law was the bond. They demanded no more, and would admit no less. It was the continent and limit of their thought.

Resurrection and Marriage

To see the full force of their question and of our Lord's reply, we must keep in mind that the whole chapter relates to the kingdom of heaven and the conditions of entrance into it. Heaven is compared to a marriage. In other places the Lord calls Himself the Bridegroom and Husband, and the church His bride and wife. Entrance to heaven, then, is gained by that union with the Lord which is called marriage, and is represented by the marriage of husband and wife.

The Lord teaches us that man was created male and female ; that when two are joined together in marriage they are not two, but one. He also prays that all who love and obey Him may be one with Him. The true relation of the soul to the Lord is the true relation of a wife to her husband. The union between the soul and the Lord is marriage in the highest, truest sense. The union of two finite souls is marriage, just in the degree that it has within it that union between the soul and the Lord which constitutes heaven. The Sadducees knew nothing of this inner and essential nature of marriage. To them it was nothing more than a civil or natural relation. And with this conception of marriage the problem they proposed was indeed difficult of solution, if there is a life after this, and if there is marriage in heaven. A woman had been married to seven brethren; whose wife is she if she passes to a world where all are living? The purpose of the question was not to prove anything in regard to marriage, but to show, as they thought, the impossibility of a future life.

You will observe, also, that there is no reference in the words of the Sadducees to the manner or the time of the resurrection. It is simply a question of the continuation of life after death. "In the resurrection" does not mean in the act of being raised up, but in the life after this. But our Lord's reply shows not only that there is a resurrection, but that for Abraham, Isaac, and Jacob it had already taken place, for to God all are living. Our Lord answers the question in a way to confound the Sadducees, as He did the Pharisees, and at the same time to state most important truths, both in regard to the resurrection and to marriage.

"Ye do err, not knowing the scriptures, nor

the power of God." They thought they understood them. They had quoted them to Him.
They failed in comprehending the true meaning
of the Scriptures, because they limited their
meaning to the letter alone. They did not admit
that they had any other than a material or purely
natural meaning. This is the cause of much re-
ligious error in the Christian world. Many of
the false doctrines which have destroyed the
church and split up its numbers into many sects
originate in giving only a literal interpretation to
Scripture. Two false doctrines most inimical to
the true knowledge of man and of his life in the
resurrection have been drawn from the letter of
the passage we are now considering. One is
that the material body is raised up from the sep-
ulchre ; and the other is that the marriage relation does not exist in heaven, neither of which
doctrines is taught by our Lord. The genuine
truth of the letter can be seen only in the light of
its higher meaning. Those who deny to Scripture
a spiritual and Divine meaning exclude the light
which is essential to a true understanding of it.
This denial is as fatal to true understanding as it

would be to limit the words we use to express our thoughts and affections, to their material meaning. For example, the literal meaning of *spirit* is "breath" or "wind." Exclude all other meaning, and what absurdities you would fall into concerning the meaning of Scripture, or of common conversation. Let us not err in the interpretation of this passage of Scripture, as the Sadducees did in the one they quoted to the Lord. Let us try to get the literal and the spiritual and true meaning of our Lord.

"For in the resurrection they neither marry, nor are given in marriage, but are as the angels of God." This is strictly and literally true of marriage, as the Sadducees understood it. They regarded marriage as a merely natural relation. It did not necessarily imply any unity of mind and heart. The parties had but little to do in the selection of a partner. This was done by parents or mutual friends. The case mentioned in the text, in which a brother was compelled in some cases by the Jewish law to marry his deceased brother's wife, is a good illustration of the entirely civil nature of the relation. No ideas or motives entered into it that were not of a material, worldly, and natural character. There can be no marriages in heaven in this sense. The answer was literally and perfectly true according to the ideas of the Sadducees.

The statement of the Lord, in its simple, literal sense, also covers a broader ground. He does not say that marriage does not exist in heaven, but that marriages are not effected there. "They neither marry nor are given in marriage." The real marriage of all souls is effected in this life. It is not a legal arrangement sanctioned by any ritual. It is a union of minds. It is the union of two beings who are the exact complements of each other, and who are so by virtue of their creation and the development of character which is effected in this world. To take an extreme case, let us suppose two infants who die as soon as born. Both, as we know, will go to heaven. But the specific qualities of their nature will be determined by their hereditary character. All creation is in ultimates. The material worlds are the workshop of the universe. All ideas, thoughts, and intellectual conceptions have their basis and specific origin in the world. The earth is the nursery of heaven. Souls are begotten here and transplanted to the paradise above, and they derive their rudimental form and nature from the earthly matrix. The first step is taken here, and the first step enters into all succeeding ones and modifies them. Through whatever experiences two human beings may subsequently pass, therefore, whatever attainments they make, to whatever influences they may be subject, the original nature derived hereditarily from parents will enter into all states, and form a powerful element in modifying them and determining the specific character of their thoughts and affections,—those qualities which will determine their eternal relations.

But this principle will be more readily seen and acknowledged when persons have lived some years in this world. The culture and development of character, the spiritual state we attain, is formed by the labor and experience and influences of this life. Those qualities which determine the soul's affinities and repulsions are distilled in the alembic of natural forms, and the wedding garments which will clothe those affections are woven in the loom of time. Every human being is to-day developing the forces which will draw him to all souls in general, and to one soul in particular, and is forming the bonds which will bind them into indissoluble unity. Now, in the life of this world, consciously or unconsciously, soul is stretching out its tendrils to soul, and they are clasping each other and becoming one. The children of this world marry and are given in marriage. The conditions are determined and the initial act of union is taken here in this life, and when death draws the veil of flesh aside, and we have put off all that is not homogeneous to our real natures, we shall see the result. When, therefore, we understand what marriage really is; when we see that the ritual or formalities of marriage are no part of the marriage itself, but that it is a real union of two beings by a process of spiritual growth and mutual assimilation, we can see that our Lord stated a universal truth when He said, "In the resurrection they neither marry, nor are given in marriage;" while He in no way asserted that the marriage relation does not exist in the resurrection.

The Sanctity of Marriage

The whole question of the relation between man and woman in the spiritual world is to be determined in another manner. It is to be decided by the nature of man as a spiritual being, by the relation of the masculine and feminine principles to each other, by the nature of marriage, and especially by a knowledge of the Sacred Scriptures in their spiritual and heavenly meaning. That those whom God joins together and makes one will live together forever, so fully accords with reason, so harmonizes with all the analogies of the universe, and is so imperatively demanded by every faculty of the will and the understanding in both man and woman, that there can be no room to doubt its truth, in the mind of any one who has any true knowledge of the relations of man and woman to each other, and of both to the Lord.

Another lesson is contained in the passage we are now considering, in regard to the union of the will and the understanding in man, and the union of man with the Lord. In a deeper sense, the resurrection here referred to is the resurrection of the soul from spiritual death. By the fall the will

and the understanding were divorced from each
other, the harmony and unity of life were destroyed, man was no longer capable of receiving
the Divine life in unperverted forms, and he became spiritually dead. The will closed against
the influx of the Divine life and the understanding
was darkened, and the whole man became spiritually divorced from the Lord and wandered so
far from Him that he was on the point of utter
ruin. To avert this calamity, and to restore man
to conjunction with Himself, the Lord assumed a
human nature, and by means of it came into the
world and reopened direct communication between Himself and the human soul. He invites
all men to come back to Him and to enter into
that relation of reciprocal unity which man possessed before the fall. He calls all men to the
heavenly marriage.

Now, it is impossible to be raised up from
death and to enter into this marriage with the
Lord except as marriage is established between a
heavenly will and a heavenly understanding in
ourselves. We must be regenerated and reborn.
The old, evil will and the false understanding

must be rejected. We must lay down that life ;
we must put on the wedding garment. When the
Lord calls us we must come. God is not our
God while we are dead. We do not acknowledge
Him as our King. And we never shall acknowledge Him until we receive His truth into our
understandings, and His love into our hearts, and
the two become united in our deeds. The marriage of the will and understanding is effected in
our natural deeds. The soul is not made new by
a knowledge of the truth, nor by the mere force
of will. No man can change the nature of his
affections, or what we sometimes call his character,
by merely willing to do it. We often wish that
we did not feel as we do. We see many evil
affections within us. We wish we could get rid
of them. But wishing and merely willing will not
effect it. We must carry the will into act. You
see, for example, a great contrariety between your
will and your understanding. You know much
better than you love to do. Now, no amount of
wishing, or willing, or desiring will ever remove
this contrariety. The marriage can be effected
only by doing. The will and understanding do

not come together in any abstract way. Affection and thought must be espoused, and the union must be consummated in the deeds of life. They must act and react upon each other. By this continual contact and mutual influence they become united. The affection becomes the life of the thought, and the thought the form of the affection. "They twain shall be one flesh." Harmony and order are gradually restored.

The resurrection of the soul from spiritual death is effected by this union, and just according to the degree of the union. The initial act of this marriage has taken place and must take place in this life ; it cannot be postponed to the other world. It must also take place before the resurrection from our natural evil state is accomplished, as the cause must always precede the effect. We cannot postpone our efforts to do well until well-doing has become natural and easy. Therefore, in every sense of the words, it is true that "in the resurrection they neither marry, nor are given in marriage, but are as the angels of God." The will and the understanding have now come into an angelic state. "Neither can they die any more :

for they are equal unto the angels; and are the children of God, being the children of the resurrection."

They are the children of God because they are born of Him. They become also, in a true sense of the word, members of the church, which is the bride, the Lamb's wife. They sustain a new relation to the Lord, because they have come into a new state. They come to the marriage-supper, and they have on the wedding garment, and they partake of the oxen and fatlings which the King has prepared. They receive the Divine love into their hearts and the Divine wisdom into their understandings, and they expand under their influence and grow into a closer unity with each other, and are drawn into a more intimate conjunction with the Lord.

The fact that the heavenly marriage must be entered into in the natural life of this world is emphasized by the Lord's words in Luke, "The children of this world marry and are given in marriage." "The children of this world," or "age," means more than people living on this earth. It means the affections and thoughts of our natural mind,

or those which lie nearest to our practical life and
conduct. It is in this plane of life that all spiritual
union takes place. The will and the understanding of the spiritual degree of the mind flow into
the truths in the natural mind, and by means of
them they become united with each other and
with the natural thoughts and affections, and they
get such a hold upon them that they can raise
them up from the grave of sin and falsity into
spiritual life. The Lord sends down the golden
chain of His love and wisdom from the highest
principles of our nature to the lowest. He weaves
link after link in each plane of the mind, of the
ideas and affections which compose that plane,
until He reaches the lowest, "the children of this
world." If there is any truth and goodness in
the natural mind to which He can link the higher
degrees ; if a spiritual affection can be united to a
natural affection, He can raise up the natural and
bring it so fully under the sphere and power of
the spiritual that it can direct and control it, and
bring it into His service. The real union, the
marriage, in all cases is effected among "the children of this world."

The Sanctity of Marriage

From these methods and principles of the Divine order we may derive the most important, practical truth, that the way, and the only way, to effect the marriage of goodness and truth in the soul and to bring all its faculties into harmony with one another, and into conjunction with the Lord, is to unite heavenly affection and thought in act. Neither thinking nor willing is sufficient. Thought and affection must be united in deeds. The moment we begin to act we get greater strength and clearer light, and find a growing affection for what we are doing. The principal reason why people generally have so little interest in spiritual subjects is that they do nothing for spiritual uses. They do not bring a heavenly life into natural act. The natural mind is left in the darkness and cold and death of a merely natural life, and all spiritual thought and affection is allowed to pass off without any effect, like heat and light from the sun which flow off into the regions of space, because they find no basis upon which to rest and from which to react. All true religion has nearly perished from the earth because it has been divorced from life. It is ulti-

mated only in the formalities of worship, and thus
is in constant danger of becoming a ritual, or
ceremony, or a creed, when it is of no value
except in the degree that it becomes a life.
Marry your spiritual thought and affection to
your deeds and in your deeds. Bring love to
God and the neighbor into your daily work, into
your social and domestic and civil life, and you
will raise them up from the servility and conflict
and death of a merely natural life; and "Thou
shalt no more be termed Forsaken; neither shall
thy land any more be termed Desolate: but thou
shalt be called Hephzi-bah [my delight is in her],
and thy land Beulah [married]; for the LORD de-
lighteth in thee, and thy land shall be married."

V.

MARRIAGE IN HEAVEN.

*" The kingdom of heaven is like unto a certain king,
which made a marriage for his son."*—MATTHEW xxii. 2.

ALL the principles concerning the origin,
nature, and sanctity of marriage that I have
already stated and illustrated tend to the conclusion that the marriage relation must exist in the
spiritual world and there find its full consummation and blessedness. If marriage is essentially the
union of minds, if it is the union of the essential
constituents of the spirit, if man was made male
and female, it follows as a logical and inevitable
consequence that these qualities and relations
must endure as long as the spirit itself.

There can be no doubt that the vague notions
that prevail in the church and the world concerning the nature of the human spirit have had a
powerful influence in establishing the common
opinion that sex and marriage pertain only to the

material body, and consequently that when that
perishes they vanish with it. This must be so if
the spirit is nothing but a formless essence, a mere
vital force without organization or substance. It
is absurd, and impossible in the nature of things,
that the conscious and reciprocal union which
constitutes the essential nature of marriage could
exist between formless essences. There could be
no masculine and feminine qualities, no distinction
of nature in such vacuity. We may go still
farther and say that there could be no man, nor
woman, nor human being. According to common notions and the general teaching of the
churches, man as a distinct, human, conscious
being is simply annihilated at the dissolution of
the material body.

But this is not the doctrine of the New Church.
According to every principle and fact of its
teachings, it declares that man as to his spirit is
organized in the human form. It is the spirit that
gives form to the body as a whole and in every
fibre and cell. The dissolution of the material
body no more affects the form of the spirit than
drawing a glove from the hand dissipates its form.

The Sanctity of Marriage

Instead of destroying the form of the spirit, or changing one of its faculties or qualities, the dissolution of the material body withdraws the veil which concealed them, brings them into view to the spiritual senses, and frees them from all hinderances to the exercise of their special faculties. The masculine and feminine natures become more distinct and manifest, and every condition of life more favorable to a genuine marriage. As our doctrines deal primarily with man as a spiritual being, they give us clear and satisfactory instruction concerning the nature of his spiritual faculties, the means of their culture and development, and the attainment of the happiness which he was created to enjoy. As marriage is an essential factor in securing or destroying his happiness in this life, we are sure that it must continue to be in the endless continuation of this life in the world to come.

I invite your attention to a more special statement of some of the rational grounds for believing that the marriage relation continues and attains its perfection in heaven, and of some of the supreme excellences which characterize it.

Marriage in Heaven

The imperishable nature of sex is a necessary consequence of its origin. If it had originated in the material body, it might perish with it. But it did not. It has its origin in the Divine nature. This is clearly taught by the Lord in the words, "So God created man in his own image, in the image of God created he him ; male and female created he them." Man—and by man is not meant one masculine person, but the human race —was created male and female, and he was created in the image of God. The distinction of sex must therefore continue forever. The masculine and feminine elements of man's nature must have been one of the particulars in which he was made in the image of God. The love which draws husband and wife together must be Divine and heavenly in its origin. When man lost that image he became divorced from the Lord, and marriage became a merely natural relation. As he regains that image the relation becomes spiritual, and the Lord calls Himself a Husband, and He calls regenerate man—the church—His bride and wife, and the relation between Him and His church a marriage. The history of humanity also uniformly testifies to the truth that the marriage relation becomes pure and sacred in the degree that man and woman become heavenly minded. Evil lusts and false principles degrade man and interpose the only obstacles that hinder a perfect union between husband and wife. As our natures become elevated by the knowledge and practice of Divine truth, all that is pure and lovely in womanhood, and all that is true and noble in manhood, is more fully developed, and the union between husband and wife becomes more intimate, and the bonds that bind them together are strengthened. As heaven descends to earth and its principles become embodied in human lives, marriage rises in the purity of its motives, and approaches more fully a heavenly state. Being Divine and heavenly in its origin, marriage becomes true and complete as man and woman become regenerate. Is it probable, therefore, that when they come fully into that state, when all that is evil and false is removed, when men and women become truly angelic, when the image and likeness of the Lord into which they were created is restored, that the love that binds

husband and wife together will be dissolved?
That would be directly contrary to the operation
of heavenly principles in this life, and subversive
of the end for which man was created. The Lord
cannot contradict and work against Himself. His
kingdom is not a kingdom divided against itself.

The dissolution of the marriage bond by the
entrance of man into heaven would be directly
contrary to all the Lord's methods of accomplishing His purposes. It would be descent from a
higher to a lower instead of ascent from a lower
to a higher state. It would be passing from a
particular, intimate, and special union to an indefinite and general one. Perfection is always attained by advancing from generals to particulars.
This is a universal law. There is a common or
general attraction between man and woman. The
masculine and feminine natures are drawn towards
each other. This common affection begins to
manifest itself in youth, between boys and girls,
and increases as they develop. It is not the love
of any particular person, at first. It is a common
affection, which leads man to see in woman, and
woman to find in man, something that awakens

more interest than they find in their own sex.
When this love is directed to one person, it
becomes exalted and intensified. Two natures
are drawn together and become one. So long as
it is a love of the sex merely, there can be
nothing of this intimate union. It is a vague, indifferent longing or want of the soul. But the
moment it becomes individualized, the soul finds
what it had been groping for, and the whole
being is filled with an intense delight, and this
delight increases, just in proportion to the purity
and interior nature of the union. When there is
a real marriage of souls, and husband and wife
have one mind and one way ; when each finds in
the other the complement of his or her own being,
the happiness of such a union is too great and interior for words to express.

Now, according to the common idea, this
intimate and personal bond is dissolved by
death, and the soul returns into a state of a
general and universal affection. Many suppose
the distinction of sex will be obliterated. The
wife and husband will be no more to each other
than any other beings. There will remain only

the common bond of love to the Lord and the neighbor. Supposing the distinction of sex to remain, men and women lose that specific and personal affection which constituted their most interior and exalted delight, and return to that indefinite and common one, which was the first blind movement of the soul towards that union of heart and life. This is the entire reversal of the Divine method of perfecting man's nature and filling his soul with the blessedness of heaven. The heavenly life, instead of being an advancement along the paths of the Divine order, reverses man's course, and leads him back to the blind and chaotic state of his first years in this life. But this cannot be. The Lord always works like Himself. Spiritual laws are immutable. Man's whole nature must be changed before he can find his highest happiness in a general affection. Every principle of his being tends to the specific and the personal. A common affection partakes more of the nature of the instinct of animals than the rational and specific forms of human love. It is therefore entirely in accordance with all the principles of man's life, and with all the methods of the Divine wisdom, that the marriage relation should remain, and the union between husband and wife should become more specific, personal, and interior ; and the more fully each one becomes the other's self, the more exalted, interior, and perfect will be their happiness.

If we regard the subject from the nature of marriage, we shall be led to the same conclusion. Marriage is essentially a union of souls. It is an interior and spiritual union. The ceremony performed by the minister or the magistrate is nothing more than the sanction of the church or of the state to the real marriage. The love that binds husband and wife together is the real marriage. This love has its origin in the Lord, and is His perpetual gift. When a man and woman find in each other the complements of their own being, God joins them together. Their thoughts and affections coalesce. There is really but one will and one understanding between them. The union is of the same nature as that which exists between the will and the understanding in each individual mind. We all know how happy we

are when we love to do what we know we ought
to do. The will and the understanding are one.
There is no conflict within ; there is no ground
for any conflict, for all the elements of our nature
perfectly blend and act in harmony. When
there is perfect harmony between the will of one
person and the understanding in another, both
natures flow together as one. Thought meets
affection and affection blends with thought in the
most particular principles. There is a blending
of life with life. God joins them together in the
beginning or in the first and inmost principles of
their being. It is impossible to separate them
without destroying the life of both. You might
as well separate the heart and lungs in the
material body, or tear the arteries and veins from
their minute and special conjunction with each
other, or pull out the nerves from the body, and
still preserve its ability to feel and serve as the
material instrument of the mind. To destroy
the marriage relation, then, would rupture the
inmost principles of our being and sever all those
ties which bind the two halves of our life together. Marriage has its seat in the spiritual

plane of life, the plane that comes out into open consciousness when we enter heaven. To destroy it, therefore, when it exists between two beings, would destroy heaven itself for them, for it would destroy all ability to receive the life of heaven. Imagine a husband and wife who have found in each other the counterparts of their own nature, who have gone through this life together sharing each other's joys and sorrows and bearing each other's burdens ; whose souls have grown together by the constant interchange of thought and affection, so that they have the same principles, the same purposes, the same methods ;—suppose husband and wife to have this unity of life broken, to lose sight of each other, or to become nothing more to each other than they are to the whole multitude of the angels ; what can they find in heaven to compensate for this loss ? Every link in life is broken. They are cut off from the attainment of heavenly happiness, because the Lord does not communicate life and blessedness to us immediately from Himself, but through others ; and by the supposition the closest and most intimate bonds of association have been severed. They are like an organ in the material body, cut off from its direct and normal connection with the heart. The possibility of happiness in heaven is destroyed.

In heaven, we are taught and love to believe, all are drawn together by mutual affinities of nature. And these are not general alone. They are personal and specific. Those who have the strongest attachment for each other are drawn the nearest to each other. Those who are the counterparts of each other come into the most intimate union. They must live one life. They must live together. They are united as the branch to the vine, as the heart to the lungs. The union is established in the order of infinite wisdom, and no circumstance, no power, no man, and no angel can put them asunder.

There is not, therefore, the slightest foundation in reason for the belief that the marriage relation will not exist in heaven. On the contrary, everything leads to the conclusion that it will. It is heavenly in its nature. It is the best type and example of that union with the Lord which constitutes heaven. It has its origin in the Lord and descends through heaven from Him. It is also in perfect harmony with man's nature in its least and greatest principles, in its lowest forms, and in its purest and most exalted state. There is not the shadow of a reason against its existence in heaven; but everything in nature, in man, in heaven, and in the Lord proves not only its existence, but its absolute necessity. It has already been shown that the words of our Lord in regard to marriage in heaven do not deny its existence, but point to the elevation and exaltation of marriage to more interior and perfect forms than those in which it has its beginning in this life.

Let us, then, inquire into the nature of the heavenly marriage, and into the relation it bears to marriage in this life.

Marriage, as has been before explained, exists in various degrees. There is merely civil or ecclesiastical marriage. By this marriage a man and woman become legally and formally husband and wife. They are joined together in this life and for things in this life. This legal bond may be the only union between them. This, as we well know, is often the case. All their natural affections, tastes, principles, and habits may be opposed to each other. They may not have anything in common but the most external and material things. Divorces are often asked on the ground of incompatibility of temper and tastes.

In addition to the civil bond of marriage there may be a natural union. The natural affections, tastes, habits, position in society, and the ends which husband and wife seek in life may be congenial and harmonious. Their lives flow on pleasantly together. Each one meets the expectations and satisfies the wants of the other. They are regarded as fortunate and happy, and, when judged by the usual standards, they are so. But the union may be confined to the natural degree of life only. It may touch no distinctly spiritual faculty.

But in marriage that is spiritual and heavenly the husband and wife are united in the inmost plane of their being. The regenerate will and understanding are married, and two lives become one life.

When the marriage is nothing more than a mere civil compact it is dissolved at death, as all bargains and merely civil compacts are. When it is spiritual and heavenly, it always remains. Death cannot touch it.

A heavenly marriage—and this is what is meant by marriage in the Sacred Scriptures—can take place only between those who become regenerated. This is evident, for only those can enter heaven. Regeneration consists in the creation of a new will and a new understanding. A man must love goodness and believe the truth, and he must bring them down into life. A heavenly will and understanding must be married in the deeds. A man must be betrothed to the Lord in righteousness, and his own nature must be a married land before he can enter heaven, or before he can be spiritually united to another being.

But with persons who become regenerated and enter heaven, those who are partners in this life may not in all cases be partners forever. This will depend entirely upon the nature of their union in this life. If the marriage was natural only, it will be dissolved ; if it was spiritual, it will remain. Married partners usually meet in the world of spirits, which is the introductory state of the other life, where their interior natures are revealed to each other ; if they are not spiritually united, they voluntarily separate, and sooner or later find those of a homogeneous nature.

Those who pass into the spiritual world in infancy and youth, and those who have never been married in this world, if they become regenerated will find those to whom they are spiritually allied, and will dwell with them in the heavens. There will be no mistakes there. There will be no alliances from mere appearances or external considerations. Marriage in the heavens is never a mere ceremony or legal union. It is a real union of souls,—of souls that are the complement of each other. As all in the heavens are drawn together by a pure and heavenly affection, those in whom the affection is the strongest will be drawn into the closest union, and will be held in it by indissoluble bonds.

That there is an innate desire or tendency in every man and woman for communion of thought and affection is confirmed by the universal testimony of individual experience and history. The more intelligent, virtuous, and pure-minded men and women become, the more interior and powerful the attractions and motives which draw them together; the bonds of marriage are more indissoluble, and the happiness which flows from it is more full, intense, and blissful. From this universal principle we may form a true, though inadequate, idea of the nature of married life in heaven.

The husband and wife will be freed from all the cares and anxieties, the labor and weariness, that must be the lot of even the most fortunate in this world. There will be no regrets for the past and no fears for the future. No fear of sickness or want, nor of any harm from any being or circumstance. There will be no fear of any misunderstanding, or estrangement, or parting. No doubts will ever arise about the reality and perpetuity of their union. They will know that they belong to each other by the constitution of their natures. If we could eliminate from married life in this world all these causes which disturb its harmonies and mar its beauty and peace, it would be heaven upon earth. But this is only a negative aspect; it is only what it is not. Let us see

what it must be from the very nature of this
union, and from the perfections of heaven.

The husband and wife will act and think and
feel and will alike in every respect, the most particular as well as the most general. They will
have everything in their dwelling itself, and everything both within and around it, that perfectly
suits and satisfies the tastes and wants of both.
There will be no differences of opinion in the
most external or the most trifling things. There
will be no ambitions or rivalries, or efforts to pass
beyond their station. They will be perfectly con-
tent with everything they possess.

The wife will be to her husband the most
beautiful and lovely of all the angels. He will
see grace in every motion and harmony in every
tone of her voice. She will be to him the perfect
embodiment of his ideal; she will be his will
clothed in its corresponding perfections and
manifest to his senses in perfect form. The husband will be to the wife the most manly and
noble of all the angels. He will be her understanding; the perfect form and expression of her
thought. He will be her highest ideal of a man.

So each one will find in the other the perfect complement of his or her own being. There will be no lack and no excess. No faculty or feature will be too much or too little pronounced. Husband and wife will have one will and one mind and one way. "They twain shall be one."

The happiness that flows from this unity of life will be inconceivably increased by the perfection of all the powers in heaven, and of all surrounding objects. Every sense will become exquisitely delicate, and every delight elevated and intensified. There may be unity without exaltation or perfection. It may be a unity of sameness. But the heavenly unity is the unity of harmonious variety. Other things being equal, happiness is in proportion to the variety of faculties that are called into activity and the interior and delicate harmonies of their action. The difference in the emotions excited in the same mind by looking over a vast waste of sand and a landscape varied with every form of natural beauty is very great. But a mind of high and various culture will find innumerable things to awaken thought and emotion which escape the observation of the ignorant. In heaven the objects of beauty and interest will be indefinitely multiplied. The faculties which they call into play are freed from the obscuring veil of flesh. The eye has a penetration and acuteness of vision, and the ear a delicate perception of sweet sounds, of which we can have only the faintest conception. And every outward object and relation is the representative form and expression of happy states within. Heavenly partners see the image of each other's thought and affection in everything without them. To the wife the image of the husband is seen in everything; to the husband the image of the wife is seen in everything. It is not alone when they look into each other's faces or hear each other's voices that their affections are awakened; their thoughts and affections and the inmost principles of their being blend in everything. Every object around them is indeed the expression of their thoughts and affections combined in one image. The wife sees the wisdom of the husband everywhere, and she rejoices in it as her own. The husband sees the wife's taste and elegance and purity and love for him everywhere. Thus everything is living with the life of both. We can all understand how much this mutual recognition of each other's life must exalt and intensify their happiness. A book or a letter that one dear to us has written, a picture which a friend has painted, a natural object that has belonged to one we love, or a landscape we have looked upon together, excites the most lively interest and awakens the most painful or delightful emotions. How full and perfect must be the happiness of heaven, where every beautiful and lovely thing is as a perfect mirror in which each married partner beholds the interior thoughts and affections of the other.

But even this might not fully and forever satisfy all the wants of the soul. If there were no progress and no variety, even heavenly men and women might grow weary of each other. Man's spiritual nature aspires towards the infinite. He will grow weary of the most perfect beauty and the most exalted states. But there is no danger of weariness in heaven from this cause. The life of every angel is continually unfolding. Every parent knows what delight the unfolding faculties of a child awaken, and from this, some idea may be gained of the pleasant surprises that will continually awaken new interest in heaven. We have only the faintest conception of the capacities of the human soul. There is no assignable limit beyond which it may not pass, and its progress increases in a continually accelerating ratio. The greater its attainments, the larger its capacity to give and receive, the more rapid and varied will be its development. Beautiful and perfect as life may be in any given state, new and more lovely scenes will continually open to the expanding mind ; new discoveries of Divine truth will awaken new thoughts and affections, which will disclose profounder depths in the nature of husband or wife. Every day will be fresh with a new life, and every new discovery will draw married partners closer together and awaken within them intenser and more profound delights. And this will be the law and the effect of their progress forever.

No one grows old in heaven. Every one grows towards the perfection of life. Those who have lived together united in heart, and have grown old and become subject to the infirmities of age in this world, throw off all the infirmities when they pass into heaven, and grow towards a state of perpetual youth. They come into a glow and fulness of life and beauty that surpass everything of earth. They grow towards a state of ever-increasing perfection in outward form and inward state, and attain a peace and blessedness that words cannot express, nor our feeble minds conceive.

Such is an imperfect statement of what the doctrines of the New Church teach concerning the nature and blessedness of marriage in heaven. Is there anything in it contrary to reason? Is there a man or a woman who does not feel conscious of the capacity for such a union and such a life? of a want that nothing else could satisfy? Can you conceive of a state or form of life that would be better adapted to our whole nature and more conducive to the most varied, profound, and exquisite happiness? The Sacred Scriptures attest the eternal nature of marriage, when they declare that God created man male and female, and that He joins husband and wife together, and that they are no more twain. The Lord's methods of accomplishing His purposes as they are manifested in the creation, with united voice confirm it, and it must be true.

What a sanctity does this truth give to the relation of husband and wife! What motives of the most weighty import it holds out to men and women to take upon themselves its vows and its responsibilities from no unworthy cause! to guard its sanctities with the most scrupulous vigilance ! And what encouragement it holds out to husbands and wives to put away from their own affections, thoughts, and conduct everything that hinders the beginning of the union in this life, and to cherish every principle that will prepare them to enter more fully into its fruition in the life to come.

In one of his " Memorable Relations," Swedenborg describes a husband and wife who had lived together in heaven since the Golden Age of humanity. He was permitted to see them, he says, that he might give to men upon the earth some idea of the life of those who have been united in heart and have passed into the heavens. When they came near, they said to him, " We are consorts ; we have lived blessed in heaven from the first age, which is called by you the Golden

Age, and in the same perpetual flower of youth
in which you now see us at this day." Swedenborg continues, "I looked at each attentively,
because I perceived that they represented marriage love in its life and in its adornment; in its
life in their faces, and in its adornment in their
clothing; for all angels are affections of love in a
human form; the ruling affection itself shines
forth from their faces, and from the affection and
according to it are their garments; wherefore, it
is said in heaven, that his own affection clothes
every one. The husband appeared of a middle
age between manhood and youth; from his eyes
shone forth a light sparkling from the wisdom of
love, from which light his face was as if interiorly
radiant, and from this radiance the skin was
throughout refulgent, whereby his whole face was
one resplendent comeliness. . . . The face of the
wife was seen by me, and was not seen; it was
seen as beauty itself, and it was not seen, because
this beauty was inexpressible; for in her face was
a splendor of flaming light, such light as the
angels of the third heaven have, and it made my
sight dim, so that I stood still. She, observing

this, addressed me, saying, 'What do you see?'
I replied, 'I see nothing but marriage love and the
form thereof; but I see, and I do not see.' At
this she turned herself obliquely from her husband
and then I could look upon her more intently.
Her eyes were bright with the light of her own
heaven, which, as was said, was flaming from the
love of wisdom; for in that heaven the wives love
their husbands from their wisdom and in it, and
husbands love their wives from and in that love
towards themselves, and thus they are made one.
Hence was her beauty which was such that no
painter could emulate and exhibit it in its form,
for his colors have no such lustre, nor can his art
express such beauty."

Such are the possibilities that lie before every
man and every woman, whatever may be our
condition or circumstances in this world. We
have only to cherish those affections which constitute genuine marriage, and make its principles
our own by making them the rule of daily life, and
we shall become sharers in a heavenly marriage
that will grow more intimate, more varied, more
harmonious, more joyful and blissful forever.

VI.

THE MARRIAGE OF THE SOUL WITH THE LORD.

"For thy Maker is thine husband."—ISAIAH liv. 5.

THE most intimate relation of the Lord to man is represented in the Sacred Scriptures by marriage. "Turn, O backsliding children, saith the LORD ; for I am married unto you." The Lord declares that He has been a husband unto His people, and that He will betroth them unto Himself forever. "Yea," He says, " I will betroth thee unto me in righteousness, and in judgment, and in loving-kindness, and in mercies." He calls Himself the Bridegroom, and the church His bride and wife. "The marriage of the Lamb is come. . . . Blessed are they which are called unto the marriage supper of the Lamb." Such is the plain teaching of Scripture.

The question to which I invite your attention is, What is the specific relation between the Lord and man which is called marriage ? Is this a mere figure of speech, or does there really exist a conjunction between the Lord and man which can fitly and truly be called a marriage? The doctrines of the New Church teach that the union between the Lord and the church is a real marriage, a marriage such as the Lord Himself declares exists between the husband and wife when they twain become one. There is in an eminent and specific sense a marriage between the Divine and human, between the Lord and man.

The idea that we attach to this relation of the Lord to man will depend upon our idea of marriage. This must be so from the nature of the human mind. The Lord employs all human relations to denote His relations to man. He says, "Whosoever shall do the will of my Father which is in heaven, the same is my brother, and sister, and mother." He seeks to reveal Himself to us through all channels, but what we receive will depend upon our understanding of the terms He employs. There is a very prevalent and essential error upon this subject, which tends to weaken the force of Divine truth and divest the terms which the Lord employs to convey it to us of their full and real meaning. When any human event or natural relation is used to communicate a Divine truth to men, it is generally supposed that the relation or event is to be understood in a figurative sense. And even when we acknowledge that there is a real correspondence between the spiritual and the natural, we make the natural the measure of the truth rather than a mere hint or suggestion of it. Thus, when the Lord calls Himself the Husband and the church His bride and wife, it is generally supposed that it is not really and fully so, but that this natural relation is employed to teach the general truth of the Lord's affection for the church ; that it does not mean marriage in its reality and fulness. But the truth is directly the reverse. The Divine truth is infinite in its fulness and in the variety of its application. When the Lord applies any human relation to Himself, it ought to be understood in an eminent sense. The human relation is only the shadow, the most general and the lowest form of that which exists in the Lord. It gives us only a glimpse and meagre outline of the real truth. The Lord calls Himself our Father, and

He is our Father in a higher, fuller, and more specific sense than any merely human being can be. When He represents His relation to the church by the relation of husband and wife, we must understand it in a pre-eminent and specific sense. He is the real and essential Husband of the church, and the union between Him and the church is the real marriage. It is the prototype and infinite fulness of marriage, of what every true marriage is in a finite degree. All marriage has its origin in the Lord, and gets its significance from Him. The union between husband and wife is the finite and imperfect representation of the union that exists in infinite perfection between the Divine love and wisdom in the Lord, and between the Divine love in the Lord and His truth in the minds and lives of men. We must not, therefore, measure and limit the union of the Lord with the church by the union between husband and wife. This human relation gives us a hint and outline of the real truth, which we may expand, exalt, and particularize to the extent of our power. The highest angel cannot rise to a perfect, exhaustive conception of it, but even we who are just beginning to learn what marriage truly is, may get some just idea of the Lord's relation to His church.

Our conception of this truth will, however, necessarily be affected by our knowledge and views of marriage. Marriage exists in various degrees, and there are very low and mercenary, and very high and pure views of it. Some regard it only as a civil relation sanctioned by human law. They think the priest or the magistrate effects the marriage. When the Lord calls Himself the Husband and the church His bride and wife, they suppose it can only be a figure of speech ; for they know they cannot hold this merely civil relation. To others marriage is a union of social and worldly interests,—of tastes, habits, culture, and natural affections. Such persons can have only a vague and imperfect idea of what the Divine and human relation is. To others marriage is a union of minds and hearts ; these can see that such a union between the Lord and man is possible, and that it must be effected before man can come into true relations to the Lord, and receive life and blessedness from Him in large and perfect measures. It is necessary to a correct knowledge of what the Lord intends to teach us by calling His relation with His church a marriage, that we gain the true, essential, and universal idea of marriage. This is the first point, therefore, that claims our attention. What is the essential principle of marriage?

It is a necessary and universal law of creation or of change in the form or state of any created thing, that two substances or forces must combine to produce any effect. New substances and forms are brought into existence by the combination of those previously existing. There is, even in inanimate nature, an image and suggestion of marriage in the fitness of substances for union with each other, and in the necessity for such union in order that new substances and forms may be produced. In the vegetable kingdom the image of marriage is more complete than in the mineral, and in the animal kingdom still more perfect. This marriage which exists throughout the natural creation has its origin in the Lord Himself. The Lord gives the ability for mutual helpfulness and union. In the lowest and the

highest forms of nature, it is He who joins two
together into one.

The bond of union in the lowest planes of
creation is affinity and attraction ; in the animal
kingdom it is a form of instinct ; between human
beings it is in general called love. This love has
various names according to its nature and application. When it is the love of the race in general, it is philanthropy ; when it is the love of our
country, it is patriotism ; when it is the love of individual men and women, it is friendship ; when
it is the love of children, it is parental love ; when
it is the love of one man and one woman for each
other, it is marriage love. That is pre-eminently
the conjoining affection. It can exist only between two who hold those specific relations to
each other, which make each the complement of
the other's being, not only in general but in
particular. It is, therefore, the highest, the most
interior, the most specific, the purest, and the
most powerful form of love. It differs from all
others as the specific affinities between two substances which force each to give up its own form
and combine in a third differ from that general

attraction which the earth exerts upon every object. This most intimate of all unions is made by the Lord the type of His union with us. He calls us friends; He calls us brethren and children; He goes farther, and calls us bride and wife.

Let us inquire into the specific nature of this conjoining or marriage love. It consists essentially in the desire and the continual effort to communicate itself and all that it possesses to others, and to be one with them. It continually seeks for the power to communicate itself. This effort is as constant and as spontaneous and as essentially its own nature as it is the nature of light to shine, or of heat to diffuse itself. It wishes all its own to be another's. It also desires to be loved by others, not so much, however, for the sake of receiving love from others as because it cannot communicate itself fully unless it is received and reciprocated.

When a husband and wife are conjoined by this love, each one desires to give himself and herself wholly to the other, to be the other's self. They twain become one, and they go forth to their daily uses of life as one. Neither desires to invade the sphere and do the duties of the other; each one desires to become perfect in his own sphere, and to do all in his or her power for the other. While, therefore, they grow more entirely one, they become more distinctly individual and personal. The unity is not gained by sameness, or by the merging of the being of the one with the other, but by distinctness. Self-love desires to be served; marriage love to serve. Self-love desires to have every one conform to it; marriage love continually breathes after conformity with the other. Self-love can only love others in itself; marriage love can only love itself in others. Self-love is only happy when receiving; marriage love when giving. Thus they are the opposites of each other in every particular. And as we all know something about self-love, we can form some idea of the nature of marriage love by remembering that it is the opposite in every respect of the love of self.

Now, the Lord's love for man is of the same nature as marriage love, though infinitely above it in strength, in purity, in tenderness, and in every quality which composes it. "There are three things," our doctrines teach us, "which constitute the essence of the Lord's love : 1. The love of others out of or without Himself; 2. The desire to be one with them ; and 3. The desire to make them happy from Himself." It is the inmost and infinite desire and constant effort of the Lord to give Himself to men, to give them His own life and blessedness in the highest and fullest degree possible. He desires to give them all His own to be their own in the fullest manner possible. The Lord never had a thought, or put forth an act, that was not intended for human good, and that was not directed to that end by infinite wisdom. There are no exceptions to this truth. Even what appears as the Lord's hostility to man and as punishment from Him ; even those sufferings which seem to us to be unmitigated evils, have their root in infinite love ; and if we could see them in all their relations, we should see that they could not be prevented or removed without causing greater evils than themselves. Within and above them all is the Lord's infinite desire to communicate Himself, and to give His own life,

His own thought, His own power, His own riches, to others in the largest, the fullest, and the most varied manner possible to infinite wisdom and infinite power.

If such is the nature of the Divine love, the Lord must seek conjunction with man. The inmost principle of His being requires such union. The Bridegroom and Husband of the church must be His appropriate name. Marriage must express the Lord's specific relation to the church better than any other human relation. It reveals the same truth so often expressed by our Lord while in the flesh,—His desire that men should be one with Him. "Abide in me, and I in you." "That they all may be one ; as thou, Father, art in me, and I in thee, that they also may be one in us . . . I in them, and thou in me, that they may be made perfect in one." This desire to give Himself to humanity, and to dwell in them and to be one with them, caused the Lord to assume a human nature and come among men in the flesh, that He might meet them everywhere, on every plane, and give to them in every form all that they could receive. He came to betroth men unto Him in righteousness, and in judgment, and in loving-kindness, and in mercies.

But this blessed truth may be seen in clearer light by looking at some of the methods which infinite wisdom has provided to carry into effect the purposes of infinite love and give of its own to others.

The Lord could not give Himself to another uncreated and infinite being, for there is no such being, and could be none besides Himself. He could not create such a being. The infinite cannot create the infinite. He could not create a being who should have life in himself. He could only create a being who should receive life from Him. So the Lord created man in His own image and likeness, and breathed into him, and continually breathes into him, the breath of life.

Man when considered in himself is nothing but an organic form, capable of receiving life from the Lord in various degrees. Man is a form to which the Lord can conjoin Himself, a form which can consciously receive and reciprocate the Divine love. If we look at ourselves with a little attention, we shall see that it is so. If we look at the

material body, we find that it is a series of organic
forms. The eye is an organic form for the reception of light, the ear for the reception of sound,
the lungs for the reception of air, the heart for
the blood. This power of reception is not inherent in the eye, or any other organ. It is the
Lord's gift to the body through the soul, which is
its life. The Lord is conjoined to the body by
an outward way, through air and light and other
material substances, and by an inward way through
the soul ; and so He gives Himself in all the fulness possible to the material body.

The soul, or spirit, is also an organic form, but
spiritual, capable of receiving spiritual life from
the Lord. It has no more life in itself than the
material body. It has no power to think or love.
All mental and spiritual activities are the effect of
the Divine love and wisdom flowing into man's
spiritual organism and setting it in motion, in the
same manner as seeing and hearing are caused by
the influx of light into the eye and of air into the
ear. The universal relation of man to the Lord,
therefore, is that of the receiver to the giver, of
the effect to the efficient cause.

While it is absolutely true that man, from the inmost principles of his being to the most external organism of the material body, is a form, and only a form, capable of receiving life, and of being made alive by the forces flowing into him from the Lord, yet the Lord so communicates this life that it seems to be inherent in man, to originate in him, and to be self-derived. Man calls it his own ; he uses it as his own, and it is his own to all intents and purposes, though momentarily derived from the Lord.

And the Lord desires to have man use life as his own. This is according to the very nature of His love. He desires to give all His own to others, not as a loan, not to place them under any obligation to Him, not for His glory, but to be their own in the fullest manner possible. He does not wish to make man a slave or a vassal, to cringe and fawn and feel mean and destitute. He wants him to be free, to know and feel that he is free.

Therefore the forces by which man is created and the consciousness of life and freedom is communicated to him come from the Lord by a way of which he has no consciousness. He is created by the Lord and endowed with life by Him, and this life comes to him by such secret paths that he has no perception in himself of its origin, and, therefore, he can use it with the same freedom as he could if it were self-derived.

Having created man and made him capable of loving and knowing, the Lord comes to him in another way and offers him love and truth, and seeks conjunction with him. He seeks to be so united with him that man's will will act in perfect harmony with the Divine will, and his understanding with the Divine wisdom. The Lord seeks conjunction with man as a spiritual being in the same manner that He seeks conjunction with him as a material being. No man creates his own eyes. The Lord creates the eye and then fills it with light. So man has no agency in the first instance in creating his understanding. The Lord creates it and then fills it with light. Man can shut his eyes against the light, and he can destroy them, if he chooses. The Lord does not compel a man to see. He only gives him the power to do it. So man can close his under-

standing against the truth, or he can so pervert
what he receives that his power of receiving the
truth is destroyed. The Lord gives man the
power to see the truth, but He does not compel
him to see it. In the same manner the Lord has
given man the power to receive His love, but He
does not compel him to do it. He gives him the
power to receive it or to reject it in freedom.
Man is not, therefore, a passive recipient of the
Divine life. There is a mutual approach, a reciprocal relation. The Lord offers man His love,
and man can voluntarily receive it and love the
Lord in return ; and when this is done there is
conjunction, union. There is a marriage. The
Lord betroths man unto Him in righteousness.
The union is of the same nature as that which
takes place between husband and wife when the
marriage is real, and not merely formal. The
Lord gains a real hold upon man. It is not
formal. It is not legal, but real. It is as real a
hold as the magnet has upon the iron, as the sun
has upon the earth, and as the earth itself has
upon all the objects upon it. According to the
degree of this power the Lord can draw man

The Sanctity of Marriage

towards Himself and pour new life into him. He
can protect him from the danger of evil and
falsity, and fill his mind with light and peace.
This is the heavenly marriage.

We must think more closely of the union
between the Lord and the soul of man, to see
what elements in the Lord and in man make
possible this intimate relation, and why it is truly
called a marriage.

The two essential elements of the Divine nature
are love and wisdom, and they are the two essential elements of man's nature. In the Lord these
two are perfectly united. They are one mutually
and reciprocally. There is no excess of one
element over the other, and they go forth hand in
hand in the creation and become embodied in it.
Man was created in the image and likeness of
God, that he might receive love and wisdom from
Him, with their blessedness. Man's will was formed
to receive the Divine love, and his understanding
the Divine wisdom. When they were received in
true order, there was the same union between
man's will and understanding that there is between the Divine love and wisdom in the Lord.

There was no excess of one over the other. They were married. Man could not think of anything which he did not love; whatever he loved, his love caused him to perceive and understand. As this love and wisdom came from the Lord and were received by man in their true form and order, they conjoined man to the Lord at the same time that they conjoined the will to the understanding in man. Truth or wisdom is the form of love, and they have a mutual affinity for each other. So long, therefore, as man received the Divine love and wisdom in their unperverted forms from the Lord, he was drawn by them to the Lord. Everything in man's nature responded to the Divine nature. He was drawn to the Lord by the love he received from Him. He was conjoined to Him; he was one with Him. There were no points of disagreement or opposition or difference in kind. Man was indeed finite and the Lord was infinite. But so far as man had any life, any affection or thought, so far as he was capable of any action, he was in perfect union with the Lord. The Divine life flowed into him, and every organic form in his will and in his understanding, from the highest to the lowest, vibrated in harmony with the inflowing life. There was no jar or discord in his whole nature. Every thought was the form of an affection, and every affection embodied itself in some perfect form. The Divine love and wisdom reached every faculty in man, penetrated it, enfolded it within and without, filled the intellect with light and the affections with love, and bound them together in heavenly union. Man's whole nature was a married land. Man was at one with the Lord. He was united to Him as the branch to the vine, and the Lord filled his whole being from centre to circumference with ineffable peace and blessedness. When the Bridegroom came, and in every form and state in which He came, man was ready, and went in with Him to the marriage.

But man fell from this state of perfection and union, and became divorced from the Lord. This conjoining love was lost, and his only connection with the Lord was by lower, more general, and circuitous paths. The higher planes of his being which were the seat of this specific conjoining love were closed. There was no conscious life in them, that reciprocated the Divine life. The Lord did not change. He did not turn away or withdraw from man. Man changed. He turned away from the Lord, and closed his mind against Him, as he closes his eyes to the light. Then, also, his will became divorced from his understanding, and the elements of his nature rose in conflict with each other. He lost his perception of truth ; his whole nature became perverted and darkened. He became spiritually blind, lame, deaf, and dumb, and every spiritual faculty was paralytic. This was the condition of humanity when our Lord came into the world, and to a great extent it is the condition of humanity to-day.

The Lord came to restore these severed relations with man, that He might give His own to man, and again live in him and be conjoined to him. He came to make an atonement, an at-one-ment, the nature of which has been strangely mistaken by man. He came to make man again at one with Him by reopening his disused and paralyzed faculties. He came to renew the marriage bond. For this reason the kingdom of heaven is compared to a marriage. The Lord sends out His servants everywhere to invite men to the wedding, that it may be furnished with guests. He came into the world that men might have life, that they might dwell in Him, and He in them.

This marriage is effected according to the laws of the Divine order. Let us see how this is. Marriage in the Lord takes place between the Divine love and the Divine wisdom. The true marriage in man takes place between the will and the understanding ; and, universally, spiritual marriage is effected between love and wisdom, or goodness and truth. Marriage between the Lord and man must be a union of truth with love. If there is no truth in the understanding, there is nothing in man to receive the Divine love and to be conjoined with it. There is nothing for the Divine love to grasp. The Lord can no more be conjoined to man while he is in evil and falsity than He can be united to a dead body or to a stone in the street. There is nothing to react to His love. There must be something inserted into man's mind or nature with which the Divine love can be united, and that is the Divine truth.

Truth is the form of love, as thought is the form
of affection. · When, therefore, the Divine truth
has been received into the understanding and become a part of man's being, there is something in
him that can receive the Lord's love and reciprocate it. So the Lord finds a lodgement in the
human soul by the truth implanted there, and the
reunion between man and the Lord begins to be
effected. It is feeble at first. The soul is bound
to the Lord only by a single thread. It will bear
but a little strain, and the Lord adjusts His power
to its strength. But when the communication is
opened the Lord increases and enlarges it. He
sends His messages of love and life along the
electric chain of the Divine truths, and excites
man to learn more truths, and so the bond grows.
We discern evils and falsities in our nature which
hinder the reception of the Divine love, and we
put them away, just as we put away those habits
of thought and life which impede our union with
those we love. As we put them away we make
room for larger measures of the Lord's love, and
we begin to reciprocate it more fully. We begin
to love the Lord, to lift up our thoughts and

affections to Him. Our love may be feeble, and our light dim, and our thought vague. But they increase in power and scope. We become united with the Lord as His love becomes united with His truth in our lives. This is what the Lord has always desired and labored for. The Lord always says to us, "All mine are thine," to the extent of our ability to receive. And we begin to say, feebly, hesitatingly, and with many lingering looks, perhaps, to the flesh-pots of Egypt, "Some of mine are thine," and as the marriage bond grows, "More of mine are thine;" and finally we can say, "All mine are thine." Then the marriage is consummated. The bride hath made herself ready.

Every genuine marriage between man and woman is a gradual process. The husband and wife grow towards each other. The woman becomes more and more a wife, and the man more and more a husband. Obstructions to their more interior and complete union are being continually put away, and new bonds are forming, and old ones are strengthening, and each desires to become more fully and unreservedly the other's.

This is a beautiful and perfect picture of the soul's marriage with the Lord ; the processes are the same, for all marriage love is a finite form of the Lord's infinite love.

We may now be able to see why the church is the Lord's bride ; for only those can receive the Lord's love who have some true knowledge of the Lord, and who try to live according to the truth which they possess. These are guests who wear the wedding garment ; they are wise virgins with oil in their vessels, and enter in with the Lord to the heavenly marriage. By the church, which is the bride, we are not to understand all who belong to the visible communion, but all who have that knowledge of the Lord, and that love for Him, of whatever name or creed, which constitute the true marriage bond. This bond is not formed by a creed, though a true creed may assist in its formation. It is not formed by excitement or passion. It can be formed only by learning what the Lord is, and loving Him for what He is ; by loving holiness, purity, innocence, and by trying in a finite degree to become perfect, as our Father in heaven is perfect. It is formed by learning the Lord's truth and doing it, till the Lord's love flows in and becomes our very life.

As we continue faithfully in this way of life, learning the truth and doing it till we love to do it, the conjoining bond between us and the Lord grows stronger. The Lord draws nearer to us and we draw nearer to Him. He communicates His life more fully, and in more interior streams, and we reciprocate that life more ardently. As we draw nearer to Him we see more of the infinite glory and beauty of the Divine truth, and our whole being glows with an intenser and more blessed life. And this approximation will go on to eternity. Every obstruction will be removed, every intellectual faculty will glow with Divine light, and our whole soul will beat as with a thousand hearts.

It is no figure of speech, therefore, to be explained away and understood in some vague and remote sense, that the bond of union between the soul and the Lord is a marriage. On the contrary, it is the highest form of marriage. It is more real, substantial, intimate, and fruitful in blessedness than any union between man and woman can be. Exalt your conceptions of the innocence, the purity, the perfection, the blessedness of marriage between the most exalted beings who are the complements of each other, and you still can form no adequate idea of what the union may be, nay, must be, in the coming eternity, between the man of the church and the Lord.

There is something in every human soul which leads it to aspire after communion and union with some other soul. How fortunate the man and the woman who find in each other those qualities which satisfy the wants of the soul! How many terrible mistakes are constantly made! How many natures are brought together by some illusion, which are utterly repellent! How many obstructions there are to the union of concordant minds! But there is a marriage which we can all attain, in which there can be no failure and no mistake; a marriage whose bonds will be as enduring as the eternal Lord; a marriage in which the soul will find every want satisfied, every aspiration attained. We can all find a Husband to whom we can pour out our inmost souls ; we can find perfect understanding, perfect sympathy, perfect patience, and an excellence, a strength, a beauty, a glory, a majesty, and an infinite love which we can respect, reverence, and adore. We can throw ourselves into His arms, rest upon His strength, and forever grow closer and closer to His infinite heart. That Husband is the Lord Jesus Christ.

www.ingramcontent.com/pod-product-compliance
Lightning Source LLC
Chambersburg PA
CBHW030606270326
41927CB00007B/1072